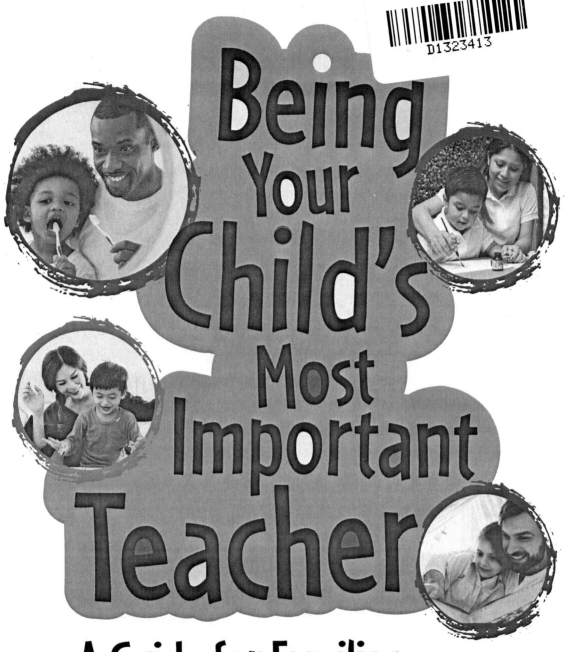

Being Your Child's Most Important Teacher

A Guide for Families with Young Children

Rebecca A. Palacios, Ph.D.

Consultant

Jodene Lynn Smith, M.A.

Publishing Credits

Corinne Burton, M.A.Ed., *Publisher*
Aubrie Nielsen, M.S.Ed., *EVP of Content Development*
Véronique Bos, *VP of Creative*
Cathy Hernandez, *Senior Content Manager*
Fabiola Sepulveda, *Junior Art Director*
David Slayton, *Assistant Editor*

Image Credits

pp. 12, 15, 21, 24, 26, 29, 38, 40, 45, 52, 56, 61, 64, 74, 78, 84, 89, 112, 116, 130, 136, 142, 145, 147, 154, 155, 174 courtesy of Rebecca A. Palacios. All other images from iStock and/or Shutterstock

A division of Teacher Created Materials
5482 Argosy Avenue
Huntington Beach, CA 92649
www.tcmpub.com/shell-education
ISBN 978-1-0876-6359-3
© 2022 Shell Educational Publishing, Inc.
Printed in USA. WOR004

Table of Contents

Table of Contents *(cont.)*

Preface

From birth, babies meet the world armed with tools such as their five senses, which help them learn about the world around them. As they grow into toddlers, children formulate thoughts, ideas, and concepts. They touch and feel the world around them—rattles, balls, books, clothing, water, and so many other things in their first eight years—drawing on experiences provided by their families or caregivers. Babies can smell their family members and recognize what they like and don't like through smell, and as they grow older, they can categorize scents. They hear the sounds around them, and they begin to classify them as loud, soft, music, or speech. They can taste the first drops of their mother's milk or formula, and as they grow older, they begin to experience different spices and textures and can begin to distinguish what they like or don't like. These beginning learning and living experiences should continue as children mature and grow.

All the experiences that young children encounter set the foundation for all their learning to come. Thus, each family becomes a child's first teacher. This most important role is pivotal for all young children.

> All the experiences that young children encounter set the foundation for all their learning to come. Thus, each family becomes a child's first teacher.

The purpose of this book is to provide families with ideas for everyday learning opportunities. Many of these activities don't cost a thing. The suggestions in this book will help support children's learning growth as they get ready for and enter school. School readiness is so important for children, and it paves the way for later success in life. All children should have positive school experiences that build up from birth by their families. I call these "early childhood prepares you for life" experiences.

I would like to tell you my story. I was born and raised in Corpus Christi, Texas, where I still live. For those who haven't been here, Corpus Christi is a beautiful city by the Corpus Christi Bay. My family has been here for five generations.

Fifty-seven years ago, our local school district was one of thousands across the country preparing to open Head Start classrooms for the first time.

I was 10 years old and looking forward to finishing fifth grade. My hair was a little longer then!

And I was precocious! When I was three, I had announced that I wanted to become a teacher. The big school down the street where my sister attended was always a magnet for me. My *abuelita* and I would walk there to pick up my sister from school, and I would stare in awe at all the wonderful, exciting things I could see.

So, you can imagine how excited I was when—about seven years after that—my mother told me about the need for volunteers to work with the young children at my elementary school. She knew about my desire to teach and wanted me to see what it would be like, and I wanted to learn about all the ways teachers work with children and prepare activities. I found myself doing the Hokey Pokey, matching pieces of lost puzzles, helping open milk cartons, and asking students questions after reading to them.

My novice teaching adventure began that summer in 1965, the first summer of Head Start. And starting with that experience, I developed a deep appreciation and respect for Head Start and every child Head Start has served. There have been so many success stories, not only for the children but also for teachers, families, the country, and volunteers.

My love for teaching and learning has increased since that time. I became a teacher, as I had dreamed of as a young child! My parents provided me with so many opportunities to learn: they gave me records with stories and songs, outdoor play opportunities, access to school clubs, and home experiences like fishing and letting me read all day long if I wanted to! I played with mud, sticks, rocks, leaves, and whatever was around my yard, and I sang songs endlessly. I didn't know at the time that my vocabulary in two languages was preparing me for a future life as a teacher—and a bilingual teacher at that!

When I became a teacher, I tried to put everything I learned into early childhood lessons. To tell you the truth, when the children would simultaneously burst into applause at the end of a lesson, it kept me going back each day to teach. I am grateful that I have been able to lead children to find their gifts and provide them with teaching and learning experiences they can carry through their lifetimes. That, for me, has been the greatest reward. My teaching career was an opportunity to meet my lifetime goal.

But I got another opportunity, and it's one I never expected. Several years ago, a friend and colleague from the National Board for Professional Teaching Standards introduced me to Age of Learning, the company designing what would become ABCmouse.com. I worked with the team at Age of Learning developing a comprehensive online curriculum for early learners, using the power of the internet to make high-quality education resources available at low cost to every child. I saw a way to teach and reach children, not just in my school community but around the world, and to help prepare the youngest learners for success early on and throughout their lives.

> The foundation you give your child will be lasting, and it will help create your child's own "early childhood prepares you for life" story.

All these learning opportunities began with my parents who knew that their little girl wanted to be a teacher and chose to help her with many experiences: piano lessons; opportunities to play outside and explore in nature, including making mud pies; fishing, beach, and zoo trips; trips to the library; and visits with extended family. Those experiences—and so many others—set the foundation for the person I am now.

My teaching adventure started 50 years ago in a Head Start classroom. It continued with 34 years of teaching in the Corpus Christi Independent School District in early childhood classrooms, and it continues today in a global way. In 1976, I did not know that one day I would have a job that had yet to be invented but would connect to everything I loved and enjoyed as a child: talking about nature and science; reading; singing; working with children, teachers, and families; and taking on new adventures!

Today, in schools, we see the need for families to continue their involvement. It is not enough to be a child's first teacher and then relinquish that role once they begin school. All children, up through their maturity, need a family's support and visibility in their schooling. Schools are not only looking at family involvement but also family engagement. There is a need for fully empowered families who can be true partners and collaborators in their children's education.

This book has two sections that will help set the stage for wonderful learning experiences for your children.

In **Section I**, the Four *E*s are introduced. They are important concepts as families rear their children, and understanding them can help families build strong foundations for their children. Children's abilities to express themselves begin when they are babies, when they cry as a signal for comfort, food, or help. Babies are ready to learn language as soon as they are born, and they develop listening and speaking skills first, then reading and writing skills during the preschool years.

Section II covers ways to incorporate learning into everyday activities and includes specific topics related to literacy, math, science, and social studies.

The final section, **Section III**, includes how to help children prepare for school. These chapters address kindergarten readiness and things families can do to help prepare children for school.

Following each chapter is a childhood story from my family, friends, and colleagues about how their families impacted who they are today and taught them lifelong skills, ideas, and concepts. The far-reaching experiences of these contributors illustrate the importance of each family member on young children. I hope that through these stories, readers will recall their own childhood stories and help bridge similar experiences for their young learners.

I also hope that this book helps provide a rich, fun time with your child. The foundation you give your child will be lasting, and it will help create your child's own "early childhood prepares you for life" story.

Enjoy your children and grandchildren!

Young Children and Learning

Parents are often so busy with the physical
rearing of children that they miss the glory
of parenthood, just as the grandeur of the
trees is lost when raking leaves.

—Marcelene Cox

The Four Es: Expression, Experiences, Explanations, Extras

> The limits of my language mean the
> limits of my world.
>
> —Ludwig Wittgenstein

The Four *Es*, *Expression*, *Experiences*, *Explanations*, and *Extras*, can help guide families in teaching their children to express themselves; in creating positive experiences where children learn over time; in providing explanations for objects, events, and experiences in their world; and in choosing extra activities that can enrich and enlighten children with a sense of wonder. The goals in this section provide guides for families, and the sample activities help families understand how to meet those goals.

Expression

Expression, or teaching children to express themselves using a rich vocabulary, is the first of the Four *Es*, as I've named them. The ability to express and use words along with a large vocabulary helps prepare children for school.

When children have a wider choice of words and expressions, they can better express their thoughts and feelings. Opportunities arise every day for adults to speak with their children, using words that describe the world around them. For example, when you shop at a grocery store, take a walk, or observe your child playing, ask them about their experiences. Create dialogue that helps your child describe the world in colors or shapes, or encourage them to ask you questions.

Developing an expressive vocabulary is crucial to reading comprehension and creative writing skills. The more your child can describe something in detail, the better their story will be. For example, your child might point to and say, "that flower." You could then ask them probing questions about it: "What color is the flower? How many petals does it have? Can you tell me more about the flower?" As the conversation progresses, encourage your child to create a story about the flower: "My flower is pink and pretty. It grows in the ground and has six green leaves and eight petals." You can also help expand the discussion by saying, "I wonder if that flower can grow anywhere." Find things to read about the flower, and look for pictures and names of other flowers to help your child learn more.

Research tells us that as adults use songs, pictures, rhyming games, and expressive talk or discourse, the better a child will be able to read. "Kindergarten readiness" is an important factor for schools and educators and it happens long before the child sets foot in a school classroom. Using books in the home, and creating a home literacy environment, is a critical part of developing the concepts, skills, and vocabulary needed to be academically successful.

The following are some ways to develop a vocabulary that's connected to a daily routine.

Goal	Sample Activities
Help your child develop a rich vocabulary.	✦ Talk to your child during cooking activities to explain the process, such as chopping, dicing, boiling, or frying, and try to use other cooking-related words. ✦ Take walking-and-talking trips to build vocabulary about what you see, touch, taste, smell, and/or hear. ✦ Read together daily, and use oral storytelling to help develop listening skills. ✦ Discuss what happens during your daily routine. ✦ Develop vocabulary about tools, shapes, names of family members, and the classification of objects, including things that roll, things you eat, and things people wear.
Help your child express forms of respect and responsibility.	✦ Model being respectful and taking responsibility. ✦ Use important related expressions, including *please, thank you*, and *may I*. ✦ Show your child how to care for people, plants, and animals. Discuss caring words, feelings, and emotions.

Goal	Sample Activities
Help your child develop an understanding of family and culture through modeling family engagement and engage them in family discussions.	✦ Attend your child's school activities and talk about them with your child. ✦ Attend special events, such as parent or grandparent events, and discuss what you did or learned with your child. ✦ Become a part of learning events where information is not only provided but families also share what they are doing at home. ✦ Develop an awareness of the richness of your culture, and teach your child about their family history.
Help your child understand that what people say aloud can also be written.	✦ Encourage your child to draw pictures and dictate stories about what they hear. ✦ Show your child how to write their name, capitalizing the first letter and using lowercase letters for the rest, such as Isabella, Caleb, Donovan, and Eva.

Expression is critical in our world. Whether you communicate through speaking, reading, writing, or listening, you're teaching your child that what they say is important—and you're taking the time to expand their world of words.

> My parents told me that education was the
> path to success—and they showed me, taking
> me to Head Start while they were pursuing
> their own college degrees.
>
> —Denise Juneau

Experiences

One of the best gifts we can give children is the ability to experience firsthand the world around them, so *experiences* is the second *E*. As children learn from experiences, they develop the ability to connect those experiences with other experiences and with language.

Children learn from experiences they have every day, including playing with toys, cooking, cleaning, taking care of pets, and going for walks. They also learn through special exposures, such as going to a farm, visiting a beach or lake, fishing, and examining how plants grow.

In this book, you will read great childhood stories from family, friends, and colleagues. You will also read about experiences that often didn't cost any money but were pivotal to the adult the child grew up to be.

As you share experiences with your child, you will gain a greater appreciation for the lifelong impact they can have on the development of your child's interests and curiosity. The broader the experiences your child has, the more they can connect to the world around them. For example, a favorite experience of many young children is playing with water. Through this experience, children get to discover that water can take a shape based on its container. When they play with water, children learn that water can be moved from one place to another. They also learn that it can spill, can be measured, it's wet, objects in it can sink and float, and many other concepts! It is a joy to watch them learn and discover with everyday objects at the water table. Children can tell stories about water after playing and will have so much more to tell based on their experiences with water. Children can play with water while standing on stools at sinks, in bathtubs, or in kiddie pools!

You can use everyday experiences as learning times. You can also create them as you go along, based on your child's interests or things happening in your home, school, or community. The more experiences your child has, the better equipped they will be for talking and writing about the world around them.

The following are some goals for developing experiences and ways to accomplish them.

Goal	Sample Activities
Have your child share their experiences.	✦ Encourage your child to draw a picture of or write about their daily experiences and retell them.
Connect daily experiences to oral language.	✦ Point out and talk about things during the day as you shop, cook, drive, read, or watch videos or TV shows.
Share your own experiences with your child.	✦ Talk to your child about the experiences you had as a child, your workday, or special occasions.
Allow your child to explore their environment.	✦ Take your child outside. While walking together, point out and discuss the features in buildings (shapes), in signs (letters and numbers), and in nature (shapes, textures, sounds, and smells).
Provide rich literacy experiences, and help your child understand what you're reading.	✦ Find time to read books daily. ✦ Make puppets for a story, and use them to act it out. ✦ Discuss the characters, details, and setting of a story. Also, discuss your child's feelings about the book. ✦ Encourage your child to point out letters, words, sentences, and paragraphs in books.

Experiences such as these will be the memories your child treasures throughout their life because they will be memories made with you.

> There's nothing that can help you
> understand your beliefs more than trying to
> explain them to an inquisitive child.
>
> —Frank A. Clark

Explanations

Children are naturally curious, and they want to know about the world around them. With their many *why* questions, children create learning opportunities for themselves. This leads to the third *E*, which is *explanations*. As a supportive family, you can respond to your child's curiosity with patience and with your time by providing explanations to their questions. These questions are an important part of your child's development. As children explore the world around them, they want to know how it works and how they fit in that world.

In the picture on page 15, a father explains the essential parts of a helicopter to his children. They knew their father worked with helicopters while in the U.S. Marines, and their questions led to important explanations about how the helicopter works. It was a very important moment. It was what teachers like to call a *teachable moment*.

When you take time to explain things, such as what's happening in your daily life, how things grow on trees, why you're dressing up for a party, or why events occur in a book, you are providing explanations that are important for your child to understand. All these explanations are teachable moments.

Once your child is in school, make sure to continue explaining things. As your child progresses through school, these explanations about many things in life—the good and the bad—will be easier for your child to understand because you will have already established communication lines and discussed them.

With the touch of a finger and the internet, you can access the answers to all sorts of questions and help prepare your child for topics ranging from geography to art.

As you go through the day, help your child understand their world by guiding them to discover and explore. Then, follow up with further explanation if needed.

The following are some examples of explanations and sample activities.

Goal	Sample Activities
Encourage *why* questions.	✦ Explain things, as best you can, with clear answers. For example: The cat has fur to keep him warm. He belongs to the mammal family, and all mammals have hair. ✦ Ask children your own *why* questions: *Why do you think that rolls? Why do you think you need that napkin? Why do people need vehicles to move from one place to another?*
Foster your child's curiosity.	✦ Play with your child, and ask questions: *What are you doing? What is harder or softer? Why is that so tall? Can you make it taller? What do you think will happen if we move this? What did you learn?* ✦ Take time to explain how things work or why you think they work the way they do. If you don't know the answer, show your child where to look for solutions, including in an encyclopedia, in a book, or on the internet. ✦ Provide materials to help your child think, such as blocks or games with rules and several steps. Also, provide things that help your child create, such as paper, crayons, markers, children's scissors, and modeling clay. ✦ Take your child to places that build curiosity and knowledge, such as a zoo, a museum, an art show, a festival, or other community events.
Describe the world around your child, and encourage your child to talk about their feelings.	✦ Encourage your child to explore the world, keeping safety in mind. ✦ Ask questions about what your child sees, hears, feels, tastes, and touches. ✦ Explain what is happening during your child's day, including the weather, seasons, clothing choices, and routines. ✦ Pay attention to your child's feelings and show them how to express feelings in appropriate ways.

You are your child's first teacher, and as you share these explanations, you will teach your child throughout their life.

> I am enough of an artist to draw freely upon my imagination. Imagination is more important than Knowledge. Knowledge is limited. Imagination encircles the world.
>
> —Albert Einstein

Extras

The fourth *E*, *extras*, includes the extra efforts and extra experiences families offer children to enrich their knowledge. These experiences take children out of the home environment and into the greater community to learn from it. With extras, children can expand their world.

Many of the extras are special places with admission fees, such as zoos, museums, sporting events, and concerts. But there are also many valuable free community programs. One of the events in my community is a cultural event that brings people from a variety of backgrounds and cultures together to sample games and foods from different places around the world. In addition, there are numerous low-cost after-school programs, based at schools, including dance, violin, soccer, and tennis, among others. These extras help develop children's understanding of rules and discipline through practice, as well as team and leadership skills. These valuable extras create a sampling of activities to help children find their interests and extend their learning from school to their after-school world.

A man in our community had a bird farm where he hatched ducklings and chicks in incubators. Children could visit the bird farm and see birds hatch, see birds in their pens, and compare how birds were the same and different from other animals. This experience was one they always remembered!

Another extra can be trips to the local auditorium to watch children's musical plays. These events help children learn about music, literature, and acting. They can tell stories or draw pictures after these activities, which is also a valuable learning experience.

The following are some ways to include extras in your routine.

Goal	Sample Activities
Encourage the involvement of multiple generations of family and rich cultural experiences.	✦ Invite relatives or extended family to talk about their backgrounds, experiences, and cultural knowledge.
Use resources to develop rich experiences and language.	✦ Utilize community resources, such as parks, museums, summer concerts, fire or police department tours, and free community events, to help build imagination, curiosity, and knowledge.
Nurture children's imaginations.	✦ During a family meeting, talk about imagination and creativity in children and why it's important. Take your child someplace where they can imagine how animals live or how people lived long ago, such as a children's interactive museum, botanical garden, planetarium, forest, beach, desert, lake, aquarium, or the mountains.
Use the public library.	✦ Explore the library, check out books, use the computer, and take advantage of the library's programs throughout the year, especially during the summer to prevent learning loss. ✦ Books will provide your child with windows into other unknown worlds, including the depths of the ocean, outer space, a different country, or the interior of the pyramids.

As your child's first teacher, the extras you provide will help your child to see the world around them in a greater light. Together, the Four Es—Expression, Experiences, Explanations, and Extras—can help pave the way to a successful school career for your child and help you work in partnership with your child's next teachers.

Education and Culture

by Erin, Senior Director

I am a woman from a lower-middle-class family in eastern rural Kansas. That is not a typical origin story for someone who has spent a third of her life educating others around the globe. However, my father gave me the gift of knowledge and culture, which forever shaped my future.

My father spent much of his life trying to find something he truly loved. He served as a corpsman in the navy, a professional chef, an amateur blacksmith, a registered nurse, an army reservist, and a physician's assistant—oh, and the bass player for a backwoods bluegrass band. It wasn't the number of professions that my father pursued but the vigor in which he chased knowledge that impacted me.

Every night growing up, I watched my father study. As he pursued knowledge and the desire to help others, I had the opportunity to watch him walk across a stage and receive a degree, not once but twice. Each night, after dinner, we read and did homework together. My father quietly instilled in me that age and gender did not matter when it came to education. Education had the power to change lives, both for yourself and everyone you might encounter.

His pursuits brought an array of people and cultures into our lives. New and diverse foods were never far from our table, and new and diverse friends were never far from our hearth. My father wanted us to see and experience everything the world had to offer because he had mined the depths of what the world could teach him and found his love of life there.

For me, education was never an abstract ideal. It was something anyone could obtain if they wanted it. The fact that I was lower-middle class was never a barrier. The fact that I was a woman was never a hurdle for me. Not a single idea was ever considered an "unclimbable mountain" when it came to pursuing knowledge. This is the gift my father gave me.

Why Do Children Ask Questions?

Curiosity is one of the permanent
and certain characteristics of a
vigorous intellect.

—Samuel Johnson

Have you ever wondered why your child asks *so many questions*? Even as adults, we question many things not in our control. For children, questions help them make sense of their world as they begin to learn about it. These questions can also spur and accelerate learning. Our adult responses are crucial and pivotal, so the bigger question is this: What's your response to the *why* questions?

Children's innate curiosity plays a large part in their *why* questions. Their curiosity about the world helps them build concepts, skills, vocabulary, and their understanding of the unknown. You can help channel their curiosity and need to know *why* so you can foster their learning in a positive way.

How do we support a young child's need to know?

When your young child is asking a question, and you know that they need to know and need to know right now, my advice is simple: you should try to provide an immediate, direct answer that's either short or detailed, depending on what you know and what your child can understand.

Sometimes, a simple, informational answer is all that's needed in the moment. For example, if your child asks, "Why does that cat have fur?" Your response can be brief and factual: "The cat has fur to keep warm. Almost all cats have fur."

This is a fully sufficient answer that will help your child learn about the world. But if you know a little more about the subject, and your child has a deeper level of interest and understanding, honor your child's interest by offering a more detailed response, such as, "The cat has fur to keep warm. He is a member of the cat family, and almost all cats have fur. Cats are mammals, just like we are, and mammals have either hair or fur. We have hair; cats have fur." You could then make it a project with your child to look up more information or borrow informational books from the library about cats or other furry animals.

You can also deepen your child's thinking if you turn the *why* question around so your child must think about it to come up with their own answer. For example, your first response to your child's question could be, "Why do you think he has fur?" Then, let your child respond with an original answer.

Getting your child to think about and answer their own *why* questions at this age is important because teachers are using *why* questions in every subject in school. Schoolchildren are being asked questions that educators call higher-order questions; that is, children are asked to read, think about what they read, and explain why they think certain things happen in the story.

Being able to answer *why* questions is also crucial because older children and adults encounter *why* questions throughout their daily lives. Additionally, in our increasingly technological and global world, our children will be asked to solve problems that will require them to think for themselves and come up with their own answers.

> Being able to answer *why* questions is also crucial because older children and adults encounter *why* questions throughout their daily lives.

Your child's first experiences in asking and answering *why* questions in their quest to understand the world are the building blocks of deep thinking and will help prepare your child for the future.

What can you do at home to foster your child's questioning abilities and support their learning? Here are a few suggestions:

- Encourage questions. Do this by responding in a supportive manner with an informative answer or another *why* question. (For example, "Why does it rain?" This is one response: "That's a great question. It rains because the clouds have moisture in them, and when they get full, it rains." Here's another response: "That's a great question. Why do you think it rains?")

- Ask many *why* questions yourself (For example, "Why do you think this soup I'm cooking needs water?") to show your child that learning is a lifelong skill.

- Read books to your child that contain many questions. (For example, *Are You My Mother?* by P.D. Eastman or *National Geographic Little Kids First Big Book of Why*)

- Post a page on your refrigerator or in your child's room, titled "My List of Questions," with the answers to why questions they have asked.

- Explore higher-order questions and learn why they're so important to children's learning.

- Talk to your child's teacher about the why questions that are being discussed at school.

The use of questions by your child should be encouraged and celebrated as your child makes sense of the world through curiosity and discovery.

Engagement in Learning: It's About What's Important to the Learner

I hear and I forget. I see and I remember.
I do and I understand.

—Confucius

What a great opportunity we have as parents and teachers to help young minds develop and grow. One of the most effective ways that we can facilitate this is by helping children identify activities, materials, and environments that are important to them, and then to focus on these to promote their engagement in learning.

What is *engagement*? According to *The Glossary of Education Reform*, student engagement is "the degree of attention, curiosity, interest, optimism, and passion that students show when they are learning or being taught, which extends to the level of motivation they have to learn and progress in their education."

Many think that children at that age have a very short attention span—and, most of the time, they would be correct. But there is one important exception: when children are engaged in learning activities that are of high interest to them. When an activity is important to the student, it can hold a young child's attention for a very long time. It is not unusual to see four-year-olds passionately focused on self-selected activities, often for 20 minutes or longer.

You can help your child develop a longer attention span and a love of learning through finding out what their natural interests are and by providing learning activities that match those interests. Several examples are on the following pages.

Educational Activities

- Create opportunities to read with your child and make reading a daily routine. Rhyming and predictable books are typically the most engaging for the youngest children. But no matter what kinds of books you read, choose books that are of high interest to your child—about subjects that they want to know more about.

- Talk to your child throughout the day, and create many opportunities to engage with peers, family members, and other adults. You can help your child increase their oral language engagement with lively and thought-provoking talks, rhymes, stories, plays, and the use of puppets.

Take advantage of learning activities in your community, such as library sessions, museum talks or shows, concerts, visits to playgrounds, and historic or cultural events. Varied and engaging community activities can help provide children with an expanded oral vocabulary and give them the opportunity to tell stories about what they did. After coming home, have your child draw what they saw, or if your child is older, have them write a story about it.

- Encourage your child to share the story during dinner or family time, post it on the refrigerator, begin a story journal, or post it in their room.

- Educational technology provides children with opportunities to learn not only basic skills in reading and math but also topics that further engage them, such as science, social studies, art, and music. Topics of high interest may be explored through high-quality programs and apps that engage children while meeting their diverse learning styles and interests. Online learning programs are extremely interactive, engaging, and fun for children.

Interactive Materials

- Allow your child to explore some of the cooking materials you're using (depending on age and safety factors), such as measuring spoons and cups, dough, and dry pasta. With these materials, they can start to measure, count, talk about shapes, and feel different textures and patterns.

- While cooking, take time to encourage your child to observe and engage their senses. Cooking is rich with opportunities for smelling, tasting, touching, hearing, and seeing.

- Create a water play area in your backyard or on your patio by using a small tub or purchasing a water table. Offer your child cups, measuring cups, colanders, and small plastic buckets to play with.

- Purchase some watercolors and let your child paint outside by placing paper on a tray and clipping it to the tray with clothespins or binder clips.

- Use a large paintbrush and water to have your child "paint" with water on a sidewalk. Encourage them to watch the water evaporate.

Environmental Engagement

- Take a short walk around your block or at the park and encourage your child to engage with what is going on around them. For example, urge your child to observe and talk about the falling leaves; to discuss animals or insects they encounter; and to describe the patterns, shapes, and textures of rocks, stones, twigs, leaves, or trees.

- Look for shapes, patterns, or letters on buildings or elsewhere in the environment. Play a game and look for a specific letter or other shape, such as the U shape in a swing, the L shape at the side of steps, a circle in a clock tower, or a square in a windowpane.

- Create learning "centers" or imaginative areas outside your home where your child can play with wood, sand, rocks, balls, swings, and other items. Let your child create a pretend fort or castle, using old sheets or blankets, with your supervision.

There are so many wonderful and simple ways to engage children in learning, just by encouraging them to notice and explore what's around them and by focusing on high-interest activities. Children's minds are the creative place where all ideas take root, and engagement helps them flourish.

Environmental Prospects

by Annalia, Senior Administrative Assistant

I was raised in a South Texas town by the bay. My house was set apart, near a migratory bird sanctuary and an American Indian memorial. Our backyard didn't have a fence. Our back door looked straight out into nature.

One evening, my parents decided that the three of us would go for a stroll on the nearby nature trail. After some small talk and pointing out various colored flowers, we came across a beautiful prickly pear cactus, or as we call it in South Texas, a nopal. Being so young, I was intimidated by the countless sharp thorns that pierced out from its sides. My mother asked me if I knew what was inside the cactus. I had no idea! Perhaps it was dry inside, being that the cactus lived in such an arid environment.

My mom looked at my dad and made a gesture for him to show me. My father bent down and pulled his keys from his pocket. He took the biggest key he had on the ring, pierced the cactus in its pad, and scooped out the inner contents for me to see—alas, it was juicy! I was genuinely intrigued to learn that the cactus had a succulent, wet, and sticky interior.

I didn't realize it then, but I took a mental snapshot of that moment. That moment taught me so much about never taking anything at face value. The thorns that a cactus bears are to protect the contents of its soft insides. Perhaps this example could be applied to other instances in life.

I learned that nature is a wonder: there's always something to learn, something to observe, and some way to grow. Over time, I became very fond of bucolic regions, and I developed a great appreciation and concern for wildlife, farmsteads, and planet Earth. I'm amazed at the diversity the world has grown. Diversity is truly a part of nature.

Though it may seem far-fetched, this beloved lesson that I learned in the presence of my parents instilled in me a profound desire to preserve all the wonders of our treasured Earth. I appreciate my mother and father for always creating learning opportunities in everything around us, even if it was just in our backyard. As it turns out, all of nature is our backyard. It's always time to learn from nature.

Oral Language Experiences for Young Learners

We Know that reading to children is a crucial step. From the beginning, babies who are read to are exposed to the cadence of language, and school-age children who read at home for 15 minutes a day are exposed to millions of words.

—Randi Weingarten

When children read, they look at the written words on a page and decide what spoken words the written words represent. But to understand what they're reading, children must know the meanings of those spoken words.

The size of a child's oral vocabulary contributes to their ability to understand what they read and their ability to sound out words, since sounding out a familiar word is much easier than sounding out a word the child has rarely or never heard.

There are many ways to develop your child's oral language skills, but keep in mind that different children learn in different ways. Here are a few approaches that are effective.

One useful approach is based on the idea that young children are very curious about the world around them. Curiosity can lead to opportunities to create valuable language experiences as you talk to your child and answer questions about the things that are present in their environment. For example, the fruits and vegetables you see at the grocery store can provide some wonderful language-building opportunities. You can talk about the different colors, textures, and sizes of the fruits and vegetables, or how they're grown. Often, there are stickers that tell you where they are from. You can point out these stickers to your child and talk about geography and the parts of the world where the fruits and vegetables were grown. And while you're at it, talk about healthy eating! Later, you can build upon this experience by reading one of the many children's books that discuss plants and their life cycles.

Having language experiences like this, which include touching, smelling, hearing, tasting, and seeing, will help your child remember the language that they have heard because it's connected to your child's senses. These language experiences also set the stage for important reading skills, such as recalling, comprehending, classifying, sequencing, and retelling stories.

Of course, you don't have to go shopping to build language. As you drive, talk about street signs, the colors of other cars, and the businesses you see along the side of the road. As you cook, talk about the ingredients you're using. When you take a walk in a park, talk about the characteristics of the people, pets, and plants you see.

When you aren't talking, sing! In addition to the vocabulary words your child can learn from songs, the rhythms and rhymes of music help them notice how words can sound similar and different. The best part is, you don't have to be a great singer to sing to and with your child—it's your language that counts.

Language experiences can be especially enriching when they're related to the culture of one's family, community, or country. For instance, when families come together to make tamales, they can talk about how the tamalada process has evolved since their great-grandmothers ground the corn to make the masa and chopped the meat for the tamales by hand or by using a hand grinder. These conversations can help your child learn that language not only describes things but is also used to share stories, feelings, and values. You can reinforce such an experience afterward by asking your child to create a drawing about it and to talk about what they have drawn.

In truth, almost any experience in a child's life can become a rich language experience—all you have to do is add the language!

If I Can Say It, I Can Dream It!

by Paula, Business Executive

I am one of eight children. We are seven sisters and one brother, and I am number six from the top. My brother is the youngest. Needless to say, I have had many teachers. My five older sisters kept an eye on me, and, for better or for worse, there was little I could do as a kid without being reprimanded by one of them. In addition to those five "young mothers," I also had a loving and wise mother who almost never reprimanded me but taught me by example.

My mother loved words. I remember her telling us about her eighth birthday when she got a dictionary as a present and read it from beginning to end in two days. I was fascinated by that! I also loved dictionaries, but I was too young to use them. They were heavy and hard to maneuver.

I also remember, on many occasions, being at the table, having lunch, and, invariably, one of my older sisters would use a word to describe a situation or feeling. My mother would kindly explain that my sister had probably meant something slightly different. My mother would then stand up, get the bulky dictionary from the shelf, and read each of the meanings aloud until the whole family agreed on which word was the most appropriate. At that point, the food might have been cold, but we were having fun. It was language first and food second.

I have been fascinated by words since I can remember. I always thought of words before going to bed, while playing in the backyard, and while walking. I used to make up words and teach them to my friends, and some of my words were adopted for some time. Others never clicked.

I started learning English when I was 11, obviously fluent in my mother tongue, and I was very impatient to learn English as quickly as I could. I would practice making full sentences in my mind. Every time I didn't know a word I needed for my sentence (and it happened all the time), I would make it up. And it worked until I would finally learn the proper word and could substitute it.

My mother's example and my fascination with words and languages helped me to learn five languages fluently and to teach four of them. I've also been able to live in countries where I enjoyed different cultures, which makes the experience of speaking those beautiful languages that much richer and more interesting. It's humbling to recognize that the spark that led to my Ph.D. in Applied Linguistics, my passion for teaching, and my corporate career was ignited so long ago—sweetly, subtly, and with so much love.

A Young Child's Approach to Learning

Learning never exhausts the mind.

—Leonardo da Vinci

It is important to pay attention not only to what we want children to learn but also to how children are learning. That's because we know that helping children become successful learners is critical—in some ways, perhaps the most important endeavor. In this chapter, we will discuss approaches to learning and social-emotional development.

Approaches to Learning

Children's attitudes toward learning can often be described in some of these ways:

- **Initiative/Curiosity:** Are they eager to learn?
- **Problem-Solving:** Can they work out a solution to a problem?
- **Persistence/Attention:** Can they work at a task and complete it?
- **Cooperation:** Can they get along with and work with others?

We call these Approaches to Learning, and as a teacher, I was always working to create opportunities for my students to develop in all four areas. Parents can do this, too! Here are some examples:

Initiative/Curiosity

- Use your child's natural curiosity. Encourage your child to ask *why* questions.
- Have your child try new activities, such as using modeling clay or rolling toy cars down cardboard ramps. Ask questions to help them wonder, such as *Why is that soft?* and *Why do you think that car goes faster when the ramp is steeper?*

- Try switching out your child's toys every few months. One way would be to take some older toys, place them in a pillowcase or box, and put them away for a while. Reintroduce the toys later, and they will seem like new. Then, help your child create new ways to play with them.

- Take your child on a nature walk, and talk about the environment to create interest in the world around them.

- Try going to a new place as often as possible. For example, go to a new museum, art center, music event, park, or library event.

Problem-Solving

- Begin with simple puzzles, and have your child work at them with you, guiding them to see the parts and the whole.

- Work a problem step by step. For example, your child might have a problem understanding how to complete a task, such as folding towels. Break the task into easier-to-follow steps by explaining what to do as you show them how to do it: "First, we fold the top half down; then, we fold this side over."

- To help develop positive problem-solving attitudes, ask imagination-building questions, such as "If you had to walk with me to the car and it started to rain, what would we do?"

Persistence/Attention

- Provide a task that requires some persistence to complete, such as putting away toys in a basket. Increase the difficulty and time needed as your child grows older. For example, have your child take care of a garden or a pet over a period of time.

- Play games that ask your child to do one, two, and then three things in a row. For example, say, "Stand up, put your hands on your head, and turn around."

- Provide activities at home that your child should be able to complete with increasing time and attention, such as putting napkins on the table and then adding utensils on the correct sides of the plates. Or, as your child gets older, encourage them to finish homework or a home task without assistance.

- Plan simple craft projects with your child. Over time, choose crafts that require a longer attention span because they require multiple steps, such as threading macaroni on a string to make a necklace.

Cooperation

- Playing with others is very important. Take your child to a public playground, interactive museum, or sports activity to help them develop cooperation skills.

- Cooperating with others includes getting along with adults as well as friends. Help your child cooperate with grandparents and other family members of varying ages.

- Read books about cooperation, sharing, getting along, and working together.

Social-Emotional Development

The way children feel about themselves impacts their approaches to learning. That's why teachers pay attention to what we call social-emotional development. This chart shows a few examples.

Self-Concept	Can your child articulate their preferences, thoughts, and feelings as well as demonstrate independence?
Emotions and Behavior	Can your child understand and express their own feelings as well as adapt to new situations?
Self-Regulation	Can your child understand their own emotions, behavior, and impulses as well as follow rules to express them appropriately?
Social Relationships	Can your child get along with others, understand their feelings, and empathize with them?

Every child has their own path to social-emotional development. Your job as a parent is to provide opportunities for development and help your child work through them, not to "push" them to develop faster.

As your young child grows and develops, their approaches to learning will become important skills and powerful strategies to become an engaged and a successful learner, willing to work with others. Your child's social-emotional development will give them a foundation of self-confidence in interactions with others that will allow them to take chances and try new things, which are essential to learning.

The good news is, you can support all these types of development by doing what comes naturally as a parent—giving your child love, encouragement, and opportunities.

Saturday Mornings with Mom

by Roseann, Assessment Director

Before I started kindergarten, my mother decided to schedule weekly "Saturday morning time." Each week, we did a shared project, looking through magazines and newspapers for an hour or two to find things "we" wanted to know more about. Then, we would research the topic to learn more.

I cut out a lot of pictures of animals and bugs the first few years and later became interested in how people from around the world lived and how they were different from (but also like) me. I acquired a lot of pen pals from interesting places, such as London, Tokyo, a small town hundreds of miles from me in Ohio, and a small town outside Paris. My mom supplemented these projects with trips to the library to locate additional information. She encouraged me to write my thoughts in a journal before I went to sleep at night. My thoughts were important to her.

As I entered middle school and progressed to high school, we began to shift our focus (less concretely) to my concerns and problems and, eventually, to national and international issues—but always with potential solutions from several points of view. We also added yearly goals and accompanied them with strategies for achieving them. This close bonding time with my mother translated into a series of scrapbooks and notebooks documenting my childhood as well as an eternal quest for learning new things, which gave me the confidence to become the independent thinker I am today. I treasure those lessons learned from another generation. The gift of directed time and interest from a parent is priceless and eternal.

Blanket Your Child with Success

It is not what you do for your children, but what you have taught them to do for themselves, that will make them successful human beings.

—Ann Landers

One of my favorite memories of my children and grandchildren is the love they had for their blankets. I'm reminded of those memories every time I come across the book *The Quilt Story*, by Tory Johnson and Tomie de Paola, about a young girl who finds a quilt that helps her feel secure in a new home.

I've also found that the image of a quilt is a good way to convey nine ideas that can help parents give their children security and confidence, not only in the present but also in the future.

The following are the nine ideas or elements, and each one can be thought of as one part of the quilt.

Experiences	Shared Reading	Shared Writing
Routines	Time	Responsibilities
Explanations	Curiosity	Imagination

The following chart has more information about each of the nine ideas—what they are and activities you can do with your child.

Element	What It Means	Things You Can Do
Experiences	Engage your children in a variety of activities. As you do so, talk to them, listen to what they have to say, and ask questions.	Share cooking time, go to the park, play games, visit relatives, go to community events, or visit museums.
Shared Reading	Take time to read together.	Rhyming books help children learn to recognize similar sounds. Story books can be retold in their own words. Nonfiction teaches about the world. When you read with your child, take time to ask and answer questions about what you're reading, and point out letters and words that your child can learn to recognize.
Shared Writing	Take time to write together.	Create a menu, a grocery list, or an invitation. Have your child draw a picture of something you did together and tell you what to write about it.
Routines	Maintain a consistent daily and weekly schedule of events.	Establish routines that your children can depend on. Create a pictorial chart for the day for young children, such as wake up, brush teeth, eat breakfast, go to school, etc.
Responsibilities	Provide opportunities for children to contribute to the maintenance of the household.	Show your child how to fold small towels, sort socks, pick up and put away toys, and place dirty clothes in a hamper.
Time	Dedicate time each day to focus on your children.	Plan for times throughout the day to talk and listen to your child, making sure your child knows that their thoughts and feelings are important.

Element	What It Means	Things You Can Do
Explanations	Take time to explain the world around your children.	Talk about what you see: the weather, the seasons, the way people feel, the life cycles of plants, animal characteristics and behaviors, etc. If your child wants to learn more about something, go to the library together to find appropriate books.
Curiosity	Encourage your child to ask *why* and *how* questions.	Help your child put things together and take them apart; allow them to ask questions. Respond not only with answers but also questions, such as *What do you think will happen if . . . ?*
Imagination	Provide children with opportunities to be thoughtfully creative and inventive.	Begin stories for your child that they have to finish. Ask questions, such as *What do you think that cloud looks like?* Encourage your child to create art or construction projects with available materials. Provide books that support thinking inventively.

These activities are comforting and enjoyable for children, and they also help build the foundation for what children need to know and do to be successful in school. For example, children will need to understand how the day is organized (routine) and what they need to do for homework (responsibilities). They'll need to read assignments and write about what they think (shared reading and writing). They'll need to explain topics they've researched (explanations) and create original presentations, stories, or art works (imagination). Your child will also need to make presentations about events and places (experiences) and investigate topics they want to find out more about (curiosity).

Altogether, this quilt of nine ideas—which I call a "blanket of success"—offers guidelines that can help any parent teach their child to do things ". . . for themselves, that will make them successful human beings."

Learning Because of Love

by Adelfino, Professor and CPA

It was in my early years in school that I realized the importance of education. My grandparents and parents both stressed how important education is for one to succeed in life. My love for my grandparents and parents inspired me to do my best in school. I came from a family of six children. Being the oldest, I saw the financial hardships of the family, and I knew that the only way to get ahead would be to get as much education as possible.

My desire to do my best in school went to another level in seventh grade. It was second period, and I saw a young girl and fell in love. When the first six-week report card was issued, one of our classmates made all As on his report card, and the girl made a huge deal about his accomplishment. Well, I knew what I had to do. I dedicated myself to achieving the same thing. To make a long story short, I had the perfect report card in the ninth grade—all As, no absences, and perfect conduct. I got her attention.

Those early years inspired me to do my best and to use the talents I was given to help inspire young people to seek their own goals in life. Today, I'm a professor of accounting at a local college. I also have my own CPA firm with my oldest daughter as a business partner.

I thank God every day for the girl I met in the seventh grade. She's been my wife for 41 years and continues to inspire me. With our five children and 12 grandchildren, there's a constant desire to inspire them and help them reach their goals.

Fine Motor Development

> Developing a child's motor skills is extremely important because motor development is the mediator of cognitive, social, and emotional development. Good motor skills predict a whole lot later in life, so it might be something that all of us should be concerned about early in a child's life.
>
> —Priscila Caçola

Once babies discover their fingers, parents are often thrilled to see their children learn to control those little fingers to grasp, pinch, or clutch in a fist. Child development experts call the process of learning to use the small muscles of the hands and fingers *fine motor development*. This includes development of both control and strength in grasping and the pincer motion (using the thumb and index finger together) and eventually in writing.

Fine motor development not only impacts learning and everyday skills, it's also an important aspect of a child's ability to engage in independent activities. Therefore, it's essential that children have opportunities at home, from birth to kindergarten, to practice using these muscles.

Here are examples of fine motor skills that children use daily:

- buttoning a shirt or coat
- zipping up pants
- snapping the snap on a pair of jeans

- tying shoelaces
- picking up a small piece of fruit with fingers

Here are examples of fine motor skills that children use at school:

- turning the pages of a book
- drawing with a crayon
- using safety scissors
- sorting small shapes into sets
- stringing beads
- using a computer tablet

Families can use similar activities to help their children practice in a play-like atmosphere. There are also objects at home that a family can use to promote practice in using the small muscles of the hand (always making sure that none of the objects chosen are choking hazards).

The following chart shows some engaging activities to try.

Activity	Parent Tips
Modeling Clay Snake	Give your child a round pat of modeling clay, and encourage them to roll the dough back and forth on the table, using their palms until it looks like a snake. Encourage your child to use their pincer grasp to pick up the snake, and then show your child how to coil the snake into a circle.
Zipping and Buttoning Time	While you're sorting laundry, give your child small towels to fold, shirts to button, and zippers to zip. For variety, use a timer to time how long it takes them to button a shirt more than once, and compare the times.
Pasta Patterns	Give your child a few varieties of dry pasta in a bowl, and ask them to make a pattern using the pasta, picking up one piece at a time.

Activity	Parent Tips
Scissor Skills	Provide your child with safety scissors, and explain what can be cut and what can't! Give your child a box lid and an old newspaper page, and show them how to cut strips of newspaper with the scissors. Then, tell your child to put all the cuttings into the box lid.
Nature Walk	Take your child on a nature walk, bringing along a bag or box to hold special items that they collect. Show your child how to use their pincer grasp to pick up items such as a special rock, a beautiful leaf, a funny-shaped stick, or an acorn. Encourage your child to put the items in the "walk box."

There are many more creative and interesting activities that can support your child's use of their small muscles throughout the day. And as you persuade your child to try these activities, you'll find that you're not only helping them develop important skills but you're also giving your child something even more important—special time with you!

Section

II

Everyday Activities

Not all classrooms have walls.

—Anonymous

Learning to Cook and Cooking to Learn

> Life is what happens to us while we are
> making other plans.
>
> —Allen Saunders

Cooking can provide wonderful opportunities to create learning experiences for children. These experiences are especially powerful because they involve all the senses: smelling, tasting, touching, hearing, and seeing—which is one reason why memories created in the kitchen can last a lifetime! With a little thought and preparation, you can use this special time to help your child build important understandings and skills in literacy, mathematics, science, health, and even art.

Before you can start cooking, you first need to gather ingredients! Planning and making lists are engaging ways to develop mathematical, literacy, and critical thinking skills because they show children the connections between our ideas and the written words and numbers that represent those ideas. Help your child create a list by providing a blank page with numbers running down the side. Include plenty of space between each number. Then, ask your child to write the word for, or draw a picture of, each item you need to collect. Don't worry about spelling or legibility. Also, be sure to have your child write how many of each item is needed, which will help them experience the use of numbers to show both sequence (numbering the list in order) and quantity (how much). There are other ways to create lists, too. For example, you can collect newspaper grocery ads with pictures of foods.

Cooking together is a perfect time to discuss family and community traditions.

Help your child find and cut out (using safety scissors!) the pictures of the items that are needed to create your meals. Then, ask them to glue the pictures next to the numbers on the list. Using scissors helps develop eye-hand coordination and strengthens the muscles used for writing.

After you shop for the items on the list and bring them home, there is still a lot more that your child can learn. Here are a few activities to try:

- Place all the items on a counter to play a sorting game, such as collecting everything that's green. For older children, collect everything that is shaped like a cylinder.

- Play a guessing game, which helps develop descriptive vocabulary, by asking such questions as "I'm thinking of something that is long and slender and light green, with little ridges down the sides. What is it?"

- Work together to create a book using the labels from cans or cartons (which reading educators call *environmental print*): (1) Carefully remove and clean the labels. (2) Slip them into clear protective pages that have been pre-punched to fit a three-ring binder. (3) Place them into a binder. When it's time to cook, bring out the binder, and ask your child to look at the pages and tell you about each kind of food.

Probably the most fun children can have in the kitchen is watching the way food changes when it's cooked. The cooking process is fascinating, and young children can observe at a safe distance, away from hot surfaces and sharp items. For example, it's amazing for your child to watch you peel, cut, and/or dice potatoes; place them into boiling water; check them for softness; observe them as soft; mash them; and once cooled, taste them!

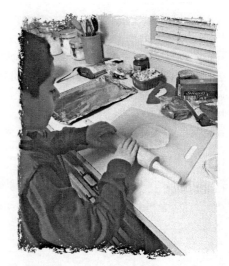

The vocabulary that you use to describe these steps can also be very interesting! Be sure to describe the way the potatoes look and feel before you cook them, using words such as *hard* and *solid*. After the potatoes are boiled and mashed, talk about how they look now, using words such as *mushy*, *squishy*, and *soft*. Guiding your child to notice that mashed potatoes are halfway between a solid and a liquid will also help them understand important science concepts around how matter is classified.

Measuring ingredients is another engaging way to build mathematics concepts and skills. Show your child your measuring spoons and cups and explain why it's important to measure the ingredients that go into a recipe. Help your child pour rice into a measuring cup and add it to the rice cooker, along with the measured water. Let them measure spices in fractions (1/2, 1/4, 1/8) of teaspoons. Your child may not completely understand what the fractions mean, but they will learn through experience that, for example, one-fourth is less than one-half; and this experience can become the foundation for understanding what those symbols mean later.

You can also try this exciting science experiment: Let your child cook a combination of ingredients of their choosing to see how it comes out (in small quantities, of course).

Cooking together is a perfect time to discuss family and community traditions. It can strengthen your child's relationships with family and community members while building a foundation for future understanding of the idea of culture, including teaching the names of foods in your family's heritage language.

Finally, consider making menu-planning a family activity because it will naturally lead into a discussion of good food choices.

Perhaps the best aspect of all is that it's a natural extension of a family activity to help your child see that reading, writing, math, social studies, science, and art—just like flour, butter, and eggs—are essential "ingredients" to great dishes.

Remembering My Grandparents (Recordando a mis abuelitos)

by Laura, Teacher

Growing up, my sister and I traveled to Mexico every summer with my grandparents. Each year, I looked forward to that 18-hour drive south into Torreon, Coahuila. I remember that the days and weeks leading up to that trip were full of excitement, thrills, and joy. We would pack our bags and the car the night before, wake up in the wee hours of the morning, and drive all day long. I can still hear the early birds chirping away in the silence of the night and the scent of the twilight morning.

As an eager little girl, I was as helpful as I could be and always full of questions: about the trip itself, our family history, our family members' ages, who were we going to visit first, and what time we would arrive. Even though this was an annual trip and the answers never changed, I would still ask! Then came the landmark questions, as those landmarks got closer and closer; and finally, I would ask the redundant questions that all children always ask, such as *Are we there yet?!*

My grandparents had a way of answering my many questions with more than just a *no* or a *yes* response. Their answers were always followed by amazing *cuentos* (stories), songs, rhymes, riddles, and facts. They used *cuentos* that we could finish off with the next word and riddles that we

already knew the answers to. The moment they said the first word, we knew the songs, and we could sing them again and again until we fell asleep in the car. What is even more beautiful to me about all this is the fact that everything they told, sang to, and recited to us was in my first language: Spanish.

Never in a million years did I think that this would impact my life as an adult. Because of all these beautiful experiences, not only were my grandparents my first teachers, but they also gave me opportunities to experience the richness and beauty of my heritage and culture.

Today, I possess a first-hand knowledge of this heritage and culture, and I share it with many of the students who walk into my classroom for the first time. I'm a dual language/bilingual teacher. What a wonderful feeling I get when I see my students' faces light up in amazement and awe as I sing "*dos y dos son cuatro y cuatro y dos son seis*" to make their first structured school experience a little easier and more welcoming. Knowing that I can do this because of my grandparents melts my heart every time—and let me add that I've learned to hold back my tears!

Music for Young Learners

Music is the universal language of mankind.

—Henry Wadsworth Longfellow

Every child's education should be well-balanced and include the fundamentals of reading, writing, mathematics, science, social studies, and the arts. The arts are often an afterthought, but they have inherent value and offer very effective ways for young children to make connections, understand ideas, and learn skills in all the other content areas, particularly the "basics" of reading, writing, and mathematics. Music, especially, is an important part of a young child's life that should be used for fun and for learning.

Songs can be used to help children learn many topics and aspects of reading, mathematics, science, and social studies. Here are a few examples:

Songs	Skill
The Alphabet Song	names and sequence of letters
The Farmer in the Dell	sequencing
Hokey Pokey	parts of the body
Home on the Range	social studies
Twinkle, Twinkle, Little Star	science
The Wheels on the Bus	describing words

These, and others like them, are songs that children love to sing again and again. This repetition is important for young learners. Additionally, the rhymes and rhythms that children hear in these songs help develop reading skills, such as recognizing words in the same word families (like *fill*, *hill*, and *will*) and identifying syllables in words.

Songs are even more fun when children can play along with their own rhythm instruments. Make a bongo out of an old oatmeal canister or put macaroni in a small paper bag and tie the bag closed to make maracas (shakers). Even clapping hands to the beat of a song makes it more fun and enhances the language experience. It's also a wonderful way for very young children to learn to count.

Music that is handed down from generation to generation is priceless and supports learning about language, heritage, culture, and social studies. Involve grandparents by asking them to teach songs from their childhoods to their grandchildren, whether in English or their native language.

Many wonderful children's books have been written about musical instruments. A favorite resource for teaching children about the different instruments is "Peter and the Wolf," a musical symphony by Sergei Prokofiev, in which the characters are represented by instruments in the orchestra.

The Gift of Music

by Daniel, Audio Engineer

When I was three years old, my grandfather bought me my first musical instrument, an acoustic guitar. He noticed that I liked to sing, and since he played the guitar and liked to sing mariachi songs, he began to nurture my musical talents by teaching me what he knew. When I was in the fourth grade, I joined the church choir, and he committed himself to making sure that I made it to all my rehearsals for the next eight years, at least until I was old enough to drive myself. When I was in the fifth grade, my school started a band class, and I signed up to play the saxophone. It was my grandfather who bought me my first saxophone, which I used all the way through high school.

My mother and my grandfather always encouraged me to pursue my interests. There have been many, so I never thought I would become a musician. Playing music was simply something I did because it was fun, just like playing basketball.

I was good at basketball, but I knew I would never make a profession out of it. My mother worked hard to put me through private school, and I had thoughts of going to college to become a suit-and-tie kind of professional, but luckily, that's not what they expected from me. Today, I'm a professional musician and a recording engineer, and it all started with that small acoustic guitar my grandfather put in my hands when I was a little boy.

Learning through Water Play

Water is the driver of nature.

—Leonardo da Vinci

Water fascinates young children. Regardless of quantities, it's always important to think about safety when water is involved and to be sure that young children are properly supervised. With this in mind, let's talk about water play!

A small bin full of water placed on a table can provide young children with hours of learning. When children are involved in water-play experiences, there is no such thing as a short attention span! Creating this kind of experience is a simple three-step process:

1. Provide objects for your child to use to explore with, such as the following:
   - plastic measuring cups that float
   - ceramic cups of similar sizes that do not float (non-fragile)
   - tubes
   - small PVC pipes
   - sieves
   - boats
   - plastic bottles
   - measuring spoons
   - feathers
   - rocks
   - funnels
   - small plastic toys

- wooden blocks
- an old-fashioned eggbeater

2. Join the fun:
   - Fill up and pour out the containers.
   - Use the measurement lines on the measuring cups to help teach words and develop language, such as *full*, *empty*, *half-full*, *1 cup*, and *2 cups*.
   - Compare objects that float with those that sink.

3. Talk about what you and your child are observing, as in these examples:
   - Since water is a liquid, it changes shape to fit whatever container it's in.
   - Some things float on water, and some things sink.
   - The way an object is shaped can help determine whether it floats or sinks.

Sometimes, step 3 is difficult to do during the activity because your child can become so engrossed that they don't have time for you! That's a good thing! Take a few pictures of your child as they play; then show them the pictures afterward and pose questions about what was happening. Having discussions like these will help your child construct understandings and learn to describe ideas, including liquid, density, buoyancy, measurement, matter, and weight—all of which are physical science concepts that they will need to understand. Your child won't necessarily be able to use or understand these words yet, but through exploration, they will have gained experience with these concepts.

Of course, these days, you don't have to limit yourself to still pictures—you can capture and present short videos that illustrate the things you want your child to observe and discuss. You also don't have to do this activity with a bin or water on a table; it can be done during bath time, followed by a conversation at bedtime.

As with many science topics, there are some wonderful children's books about water; one of my favorites is *Water's Way* by Lisa Westberg Peters. Share this book with your child to help develop their understanding about evaporation, condensation, erosion, and how water flows through text and pictures designed for a young child's reading level.

The following chart has more ideas for water explorations.

Activity	Parent Tips
"Paint" with Water	Place a small amount of water in a plastic bowl. Give your child a thick paintbrush, and tell them to "paint" with water on the sidewalk, at the park, or on a concrete slab in your backyard. Discuss the "disappearing" pictures or letters, which can be a wonderful introduction to a discussion about evaporation!
Bubbles	Buy an eggbeater or hand mixer at the dollar store. Have your child play with bubbles by placing dish detergent in a large bin and using the beater to make lots of bubbles. This will also provide hand coordination practice for your child!
Ice Cubes	Place ice cubes on a napkin, and have your child watch the ice melt. Have them hold the cube for a minute or so and discuss how their warm hand makes the ice melt faster.
Floating and Sinking	During bath time, talk about sponges and how they absorb water. Compare and contrast the sponge with a bar of soap, which does not absorb water. Compare whether both can float. Try floating and sinking other objects. Ask questions about why your child thinks this happens and how weight and shape can make a difference.

Remember, you don't have to be a science teacher to teach concepts like these to your child. All you have to do is create an environment with interesting things to explore and objects to explore with. Put your child in the environment and become curious and interested in what they see, hear, and touch, and explore right along with them. As you do this, you will be planting seeds of understanding about physical science concepts that your child will soon formally encounter in school.

Crab Island

by Nicole, Teacher

Some families have that spot or special place that inspires and rejuvenates them. As a child, and now for my own young children, that place is Crab Island. Crab Island is a group of boulders located where the sand meets the shore in Green Hill Beach, Rhode Island. I've learned so many lessons at Crab Island that I continue to pass on to my little boys and my students, from math to athletics.

It wasn't until I was an adult that I realized the tremendous value of the balance and mobility it takes to physically navigate Crab Island—it inspires our yoga practice! We collect and sort rocks and other hidden treasures, and we identify, observe, and learn respect for marine life. Inspired by a children's book, I once carried 50 rocks across state lines so my students could paint to demonstrate their uniqueness. Often, when I sit down to write, I draw inspiration from Crab Island—the roar of the ocean, the smell of salt air, and the feeling of freedom that comes from exploration.

I recently read an article that argued children might be experiencing more sensory processing issues due to not being out in nature with the freedom to explore. I'm professionally and personally interested in this topic, and I can't help but think about Crab Island. I've observed my children and other neighborhood kids as they've used their autonomy to risk standing on slippery rocks to reach into the water. What I've noticed most is that these children—without a care in the world—are connecting across age spans while learning lifelong social and academic skills that go beyond a textbook or a screen. It's amazing that the special place I cherished as a child is still like a fountain, providing me with new lessons and perspectives!

Drawing for Young Learners

Drawing is like making an expressive gesture
with the advantage of permanence.

—Henri Matisse

Children's drawings are proof of the incredible imaginations and creativity young children possess!

When I was a classroom teacher, I created hand-drawn pictures of what my students were going to learn. This showed them that we can communicate through drawing, just like book illustrators do. Then, I showed them that those pictures can be described by words, and we can read them. This also showed the children that I was not afraid to draw, no matter what it looked like. I just did my best. What was important for the children to learn was that drawing is a way to express oneself; and after seeing me draw, not once did they say that they couldn't draw! This was a crucial turning point in encouraging their learning and creativity.

Drawing promotes recognition of visual details, conceptual understanding of what is being learned, and improved eye-hand coordination. The children with detailed drawings became the best writers of the alphabet letters. My four-year-old students amazed me! Their drawings showed many details of the concepts we were studying. During a theme on insect families, their renderings of butterflies, ladybugs, flies, and other insects had heads, thoraxes, abdomens, and the correct number of legs!

Drawing promotes recognition of visual details, conceptual understanding of what is being learned, and improved eye-hand coordination.

At home, ask your child to draw what they did that day. Or ask your child to draw pictures of family members or friends. You can also make drawing a family project: draw part of a picture, and ask your child to add to it. Share those pictures by posting them on the refrigerator.

Be sure to encourage your child to draw as much as possible every day. Keep a scrapbook of their drawings as a gift for grandparents.

As your child begins to learn to write letters, you can ask them to write labels and captions for the drawings. Don't worry about spelling and legibility—what's important is that your child is making connections between pictures, words, and ideas.

All these activities will show your child that you value their written communications—a valuable step along the road to learning to write.

Fueling Wonder

by Alex, Artist

As a child, I was always fascinated by cinema. Whether it was an amusement park filled with prehistoric dinosaurs or wars in a faraway galaxy, these imaginary stories enthralled me, inadvertently fueling my sense of wonder. I can recall playing with my action figures and reenacting scenes from my favorite films, and crudely drawing characters from said films.

My father, Jaime, also loved movies. We would have movie marathons on weekends, and as I aged, the experience evolved from watching movies at home to going to the theater. Whether the movie was good or bad, my father never cared. He just smiled as we were both swept away by some new, unknown adventure.

At seven years old, I told my dad that I wanted to make movies when I grew up. He told me that I could do anything I put my mind to if I worked hard and went to school. I put my nose to the grindstone and began to draw and write vigorously. My dad would indulge me by listening to any story I wrote or watching any play I put on with my action figures. I was grateful to have an audience, even if it was only my dad.

Fast-forward 18 years. My life has changed immensely since I was a child. I graduated from California State University, Los Angeles, with a degree in Animation and a minor in Communications. Furthermore, my animated thesis film was accepted into three film festivals, and I'm currently directing my first live-action feature film, which I also wrote. Although my father is no longer with us, I will never forget that his support of my passion, starting in my childhood, made me who I am today. For that, I'm eternally grateful.

Outdoor Play for Young Learners

Children should play outside and get dirty.
—National Trust

Did you go outside and play when you were a young child? Did you love that special time of freedom to look at leaves, play with pets, spend time with friends, or simply lie down and look at the sky?

Many young children today don't have that opportunity. Through the years, we've lost some of that freedom we had when our parents opened the door and told us to go outside and play. It was our chance to use our imaginations, jump rope, play jacks, play ball, play with toys outside, or do whatever we wanted to do. It was our own time until we were called for lunch or dinner. Most of us can't even imagine doing that today! It's natural to want to keep our children safe. So, what can we do to enhance children's outdoor play and keep them safe yet give them a sense of play freedom?

Step back and provide supervised yet uninterrupted time for children to be children. They should be able to exercise their large muscles by jumping, throwing a ball, skipping, riding a bike, or pushing someone else on a swing and taking turns swinging.

We know that these kinds of activities benefit children in many ways because they help children:

- develop eye-hand coordination;
- increase flexibility of movement;
- exercise the imagination with pretend play;
- learn to negotiate rules with other children; and
- follow rules that they have negotiated with other children.

Active play is also a partner to literacy. Reading stories helps fuel children's imaginations as they create games and improvise dialogue for their characters, for example: a box becomes a pirate ship or a table for a tea party, a fenced yard becomes a castle tower, and a tree becomes a forest.

Here are a few favorite books to read with your child to help inspire their outdoor play:

- *Go Out and Play* by Adam Ciccio
- *A Rainbow of My Own* by Don Freeman
- *We're Going on a Leaf Hunt* by Steve Metzger
- *We're Going on a Bear Hunt* by Michael Rosen
- *Where the Wild Things Are* by Maurice Sendak
- *Seasons of Joy: Every Day Is for Outdoor Play* by Claudia Marie Lenart
- *Let's Play Outside* by Pat Rumbaugh
- *Lucia the Luchadora* by Cynthia Leonor Garza

Props can help, too. Little plastic containers can be used to make castles. Small bins can hold water for playing with toy boats or floating and sinking objects. Leaves can decorate mud cakes and pies. And dirt, sand, and snow can provide for limitless creative outdoor opportunities!

A small investment in equipment can go a long way. A piece of chalk creates a hopscotch court and a motivation for exercise that improves strength and balance. A ball and a wall or a set of jacks develop coordination and concentration skills. A jump rope can lead to many hours of physical development, with the introduction of jumping rope rhymes to support an improved sense of word sounds and rhythm:

> *Teddy Bear, Teddy Bear, turn around.*
> *Teddy Bear, Teddy Bear, touch the ground.*
> *Teddy Bear, Teddy Bear, touch your shoe.*
> *Teddy Bear, Teddy Bear, that's all for you!*

Of course, if you aren't certain your child is playing in a protected area under the supervision of someone you trust, then you'll want to be there. But stay in the background and don't intervene to settle arguments, except as a last resort, so your child can develop their own negotiation skills.

One thing you can do is take pictures; then later, put them in a scrapbook with captions that you and your child write together. Your child might pick up the wonderful habit of journaling as they get older! And in any case, you'll have the scrapbook to share together for years to come—and for your child to use to introduce their children to the joys of outdoor play.

The most important thing to remember is that nothing takes the place of outdoor play, where your child's imagination can "run wild" as well!

It's Cold Out Here!

by Daniel, Software Engineer

When I was 10, my family went to Fenway Park to see the Red Sox play the Orioles. It was my first time at Fenway Park. I was always a baseball fan, collecting baseball cards, but it was awe-inspiring to see my favorite players playing right there on the field! I became a hard-core Red Sox fan that day, and my obsession with all things Boston and all things sports only continued to grow.

Growing up in Maine, there were more moose than people. We lived on a military base, and every weekend and during the summer, my mom would kick me out of the house all day, every day, to play outside with the neighbors. We played wiffle ball and hockey in the street, we played football and soccer, and we sledded down the mountainside. I can remember trying to play soccer or football when the ground was frozen. Slide tackles really hurt on those days. I also played the "sport of the season" throughout the year—baseball in the spring, soccer in the fall, and basketball in the winter.

As a child, I would complain about having to go outside all the time, but as an adult, I can see how much it shaped my life. I love sports so much that I subscribe to MLB, NBA, and ESPN, and probably watch about 145 games a year. As a dad, I'm dying for one of my kids to latch on to sports. I try to get them involved by taking them to baseball games and different sporting events and signing them up for the sport of the season. We also play a lot at home and have the sporting equipment for basketball, T-ball, golf, tennis, badminton, soccer, cycling, ultimate frisbee, and hiking—you name it, we have it. Although my kids show little interest now, I hope as they get older they'll share my passion for sports. Go, Red Sox!

Inspiring Creativity in Young Children

You see a child play, and it is so close to seeing an artist paint, for in play a child says things without uttering a word. You can see how he solves his problems. You can also see what's wrong. Young children, especially, have enormous creativity, and whatever's in them rises to the surface in free play.

—Erik Erikson

Sometimes, as I showed my four-year-old students some new materials to work with, which teachers call *manipulatives*, the children would ask me, "What does it do?" This question made me think about what we give children to play with: too often, they're toys and manipulatives that are designed to "do" something interesting but don't require the child to "do" very much at all!

Favorite choices for manipulatives have always been open-ended materials. These are materials that require children to think and construct for themselves. Examples include blocks, geometric shapes, modeling clay, paint, and other materials that allow for creating or building without much instruction or guidance.

Here's an example of an activity I have done based on the book *Cuckoo* by Lois Ehlert (a Mexican folktale). This book features beautiful folk art and vivid colors, much like the tinwork and cutout fiesta flag banners of Mexico. After reading the story, I gave my students a collection of paper shapes cut from construction paper and asked them to design their own cuckoo. We talked about geometric shapes, colors, and how birds have certain body parts. The children created amazing birds! None of the resulting original works of art looked the same, and all were beautiful. The children were proud of their creations. And the conversations we had during this process were rich in vocabulary.

The students were then inspired to try and create birds using plastic construction pieces and unit blocks. They also painted birds on the painting easel and used feathers and pasta to create more birds.

These open-ended materials did not "do" anything, but they could be used in a creative way to inspire the child to "do." In the end, students experienced a wonderful piece of children's literature, discovered some science content that became more interesting and relevant to them by its relationship to that story: how birds look, what they do, what they eat, where they live, and how they can be represented. Additionally, they learned more names and characteristics of basic shapes and how to work with different mediums to create artistic pieces.

What can you do as a parent? Look for toys and think of projects that allow your child to be creative and to construct, even though they might be slightly messy endeavors. (An old shower curtain liner on the floor helps protect the floor from any spills, glue, or paint.) And try to think about the things that are already in your home that can be used as inspirations for creativity.

While you're cooking, for example, your child can arrange macaroni into interesting patterns. Multicolored lentils and beans can become interesting designs, and a little glue turns those designs into something they can hang on a wall. (Always remember, though, not to give such small objects to very young children.) Modeling clay is the perfect manipulative to keep your child occupied while you're preparing meals, as your child can "make" a pizza, bread, chicken, or a pie. It's easy to make your own play dough, and there are many recipes available on the internet.

Remember, the best manipulatives aren't always found inside—they're outside, provided by nature. I truly believe that my creativity was originally encouraged and inspired by my ability to make awesome mud cakes, decorated with leaves from our backyard tree.

In a world where technology does so much for us—including many jobs that were once done by people—the ability to be creative may be your child's most important future asset. So, the next time you're in the toy aisle, ask yourself: *what will inspire my child to "do"?*

From Light to Art

by Alyssia, Organizational Manager

Light can be used in many ways. My mom used it under a small piece of plexiglass as a temporary lightboard when she was writing calligraphy. As a child, I can remember her sitting at our kitchen table, addressing 200 or more invitations by hand, one by one. A dying art! She would also write my name in my books and on other special things. In a family of five kids, it's good to have your name on things! As I watched her, I was so fascinated by what could be accomplished with paper and pen—and a little bit anxious that she might make a mistake! If she did, she would always make it a fancy part of the letter, so it added to the creativity of the piece and became completely unnoticeable. She would let me use the pens too, and she showed me how to hold them at the right angle to achieve the right look. I still use the letter *A* she taught me in my signature today.

As an adult, I can see that my interest in art and design stemmed from this experience. Calligraphy takes practice, precision, patience, and creativity. My mom has all of that, and thankfully, I think it rubbed off on me. It has led me to create art in a different way, through my studies and work in graphic design and art direction. Now, I'm able to create many different types of designs, combining typography with illustrations, photos, and effects to create that "just right" look. Admittedly, it's not as painstaking as calligraphy, but I love it.

Seeing creativity at a young age opened this door for me, allowing me to make it my own and create again and again. I hope to one day learn how to do calligraphy like my mom and keep that art alive in this digital age. I'm so thankful for my creative beginning and what it has led to in my life. I hope it can be passed down through me to my children and to those around me.

The Allure of Technology for Young Learners

I genuinely believe that we have an opportunity to revolutionize how we educate our children.

—LeVar Burton

As children look around their environment today, they're seeing not only the natural world but also an increasingly technological world. Even classrooms are equipped with technology we never dreamed possible when we were growing up. For adults, this new world of technology makes possible instant connections between people, information, and ideas. But for parents with young children who are often attracted to digital devices, technology may also raise questions and concerns for their children.

Many child development experts worry that too much time passively consuming entertainment media can limit a child's opportunities to play and interact with others. There's also the concern that too much screen time can contribute to health issues, such as obesity, by reducing a child's daily movement and exercise, while offering little value in return.

Children learn best when we help them make connections between the world around them and what they see and hear on the screen.

The good news is that there are many active and educational applications of technology that can be beneficial for your child.

It boils down to balance. Children need a balance of activities, including lots of physical play and movement. They also need learning and reading that does not include screen time; healthy routines for eating, sleeping, and hygiene; along with age-appropriate, education-focused screen time with adult oversight and monitoring.

Education technology has a lot to offer your child. Digital resources can be very helpful for their learning of language, concepts, and skills. But for every appropriate and effective app or website, there are many more that are not quality programs or applications.

How do you decide which education technology resource to use? Here are the questions you can ask yourself (you're looking for as many *yes* answers as possible):

- Does the site teach a particular objective? Does it help your child develop a language, reading, or math skill?

- Is there an opportunity for your child to interact with the program and share what they are doing with others?

- Are there high-quality graphics? Are the pictures clearly illustrated with details that your child can learn from?

- Is the print big enough for your child to read easily?

- Is it voiced so your child can learn vocabulary, concepts, and skills by listening?

- Is it engaging? Will your child use it more and learn more because it's fun?

- Does it promote thinking, creativity, and play?

- Are there parent tips for the activities so that families can learn together?

Once you've decided to let your child use technology, you should continually monitor their use; and if your child is in preschool, sit with them to establish a learning connection that will last. To get the most benefit from the experience, ask your child questions. The following chart offers suggested questions.

If your child is listening to nursery rhymes on a phone or tablet app . . .	. . . ask which words rhyme.
If your child is counting numbers . . .	. . . ask them to show you the amounts for the numbers seen on the screen, using real objects such as pencils, blocks, or small toys.
If your child is learning colors through an app . . .	. . . ask them to match a particular color to something in the room.
If your child is reading an online book . . .	. . . ask what the story is about, who is in the story, and where the story takes place. Responding will help develop their language skills.

Screen-based devices will continue to attract children, and high-quality education technology can offer engaging and effective learning experiences with those devices. We need to remember that technology has limits. It's our job to create a supportive real-world learning environment, establish a daily routine that promotes learning, and regularly interact with our young learners in ways that will help them build their vocabulary and master other essential early learning concepts and skills.

Children learn best when we help them make connections between the world around them and what they see and hear on the screen.

Not Bored with Board Games

by Michele, Teacher

When I was growing up in the '70s, board games were a staple in our home. I remember playing Trouble with my cousin and trying to decide if I should land on him and send him back home so I could win or skip over him so he wouldn't get mad! I was practicing decision-making skills and becoming competitive as I finally decided to land on his head so I could win!

One of my most favorite board game memories is playing Monopoly on Friday nights. I remember being about six or seven years old when I was introduced to this colorful multipiece game. My parents were my opponents, but I had to be humble because they were still the bosses of me!

I was a pretty good reader at the time, but math was not my strength by any means. With an accountant for a dad, I am sure he looked at this game as the best opportunity for me to learn math in a fun way, and he quietly hoped for a future financial mind! I liked playing outside, but the most meaningful memories of my childhood are the times when my parents stopped being grown-ups and simply played with me. No cellphones, no devices, no television—just them, our board games, and me!

As I continued to play Monopoly, I learned how to count money, and I even learned some geography based on real locations. Of course, I had to read everything, which helped my fluency and vocabulary skills! I learned that learning could be fun and bring people together.

My parents would say that you can learn something new every day, even when you play! This concept has helped shape how I interact with my son, who has been playing board games since he was two. I continue to enjoy board games with my family!

Books, Books, Books!

> There are many little ways to enlarge your child's world. Love of books is the best of all.
>
> —Jacqueline Kennedy Onassis

Open a book with your child, and step into another world!

When we give children the gift of books and language, we provide them with imaginative experiences that are important parts of building a nation of creative thinkers and innovators.

Early experiences with quality children's literature help build oral vocabulary, which is a critical component of learning how to read. Building oral language vocabulary is just one of the ways that books help young children. Through exposure to books, children also learn that what people think can be written down, that those squiggly things are letters, and that the letters represent the sounds that make up words. In the process of teaching these and other reading skills and concepts, the selection of high-quality and high-interest books is also very important. Many parents wonder, *How do I know which books to select?*

One resource that can help you choose children's books is Reading Rockets, a national multimedia literacy initiative that offers information and resources on how young children learn to read. The Children's Book Council (**www.readingrockets.org/article/choosing-childs-book**) provides guidelines for book selections for babies and toddlers, preschoolers and kindergarteners, children in the early school years (ages five to eight), and older children (ages nine and up).

Stories are wonderful vehicles for introducing children to new worlds.

High-interest books for children in the early years share these qualities:

- They have a good rhythm.
- They're predictable.
- They have things in them that children can relate to.
- They describe experiences that mirror children's own, with elements such as families and pets and daily activities such as eating, playing, and learning.

Many Mother Goose books and nursery rhymes are helpful because their rhythms and rhymes familiarize children with how words can sound similar and different. When children are hearing and learning such rhymes, it can be a big help to have accompanying hand movements, as with the rhyme Pat-a-Cake.

Stories are wonderful vehicles for introducing children to new worlds. Likewise, nonfiction books show them the rich variety and wonders of the real world that they'll someday be able to explore. Offer your child lots of choices as you select nonfiction topics, whether it's different vehicles and how they move; the animals that live under the sea; the lives of insects; or how people live in the desert, tundra, or rainforest. If you see your child exhibiting a special interest in a particular topic, look for similar books on the topic to help further expand their knowledge.

The books that you share with your child can also provide opportunities to teach these important book concepts:

- We read from top to bottom and left to right.
- Books have authors and illustrators.
- What we read can be reread because the words are written.
- Illustrations help us understand what's being said in the story.
- We should take care of books.

The first time, or the first few times, you share a book with your child, you'll probably want to read the book all the way through for enjoyment, answering questions as your child poses them.

During subsequent readings, you may want to pause to ask questions like these to help your child learn to think about what they are hearing:

- Who is in the story? Are they people or animals?
- Where does the story take place?
- What happened first, second, and third in the story?
- What was your favorite part?
- Can you find specific letters? For example, can you find any letters on this page that are also in your name?
- What is the author's name?
- Is there another book that we read that's written by this author?
- Who is the illustrator?
- What word on this page sounds like *blue*? (Yes, the word *blew*!)
- What word on this page rhymes with *pig*? (Yes, the word *big*!)
- Can you help me read the book now?

When you and your child read a book together and talk about it in these ways, you are creating what reading experts call *shared reading experiences*. Such experiences provide a background for developing your child's understanding of the alphabetic principle—the basic idea that the words we speak and listen to are represented in writing, with letters that stand for the sounds in those words. Understanding the alphabetic principle is a critical and necessary step on your child's path to learning to read.

Share books early, share books often, and make each reading experience a pleasure for both you and your child. If you do this, you'll be successful in one of your most important responsibilities as your child's first teacher.

My Mother's Books and Me

by John, Lexicographer

Long before I learned to read, I became fascinated by books. When I could barely walk, I would sit and pretend to read the Reader's Digest because it was small, and I could hold it the way I saw my mother hold her books when she was reading. Sometimes, I would look at her books, turn the pages, and make up what they said. I still have one of her favorite books, a book of stories and cartoons (for grown-ups) that also became one of my favorites (*The Thurber Carnival*, which I recommend to everyone). I know I read it—I mean, I know I looked at it—when I was two or three years old because many pages are covered with my crayon and pencil scribbles. I guess I read it when my mother wasn't looking! Maybe I even thought I was writing in it.

I loved it when my mother would read to my sister and me. She would make all the right animal sounds and make the characters in our children's books sound as real, as scary, or as funny as could be. I also liked to look at the books on her bookshelves: books about art and travel, history, and biographies. As I began to learn to read, I loved trying to read those books, even if I didn't understand everything I was reading. From kindergarten through fourth grade, I would go back to them again and again.

Many, many years later, I can still remember some of the pictures and stories, but mostly, I remember the comfortable way those books made me feel. I could be in a different place or a different time, and no one else would ever know what that was like for me. Perhaps best of all, my mother didn't try to make me read, and she didn't try to stop me from reading her books. I don't know if she knew I was reading them, but I'm sure she did. (You know how mothers pay attention!) And later, as an adult, when I read those books more carefully, it was like going back to a familiar place that still had lots to teach me.

Those early experiences of reading books that were way beyond my understanding must have sparked my curiosity about things in a particularly "bookish" sort of way. I'm sure they're an important part of the reason I became a literature professor and dictionary writer. My mother hadn't gone to college, but after I finished college, she started college and graduated when she was 55 years old. Her home was always filled with books, just as my home is not only filled but overflowing with them. Even so, I still love to get new books.

Take Your Young Child to the Library!

A book is a dream that you hold
in your hands.

—Neil Gaiman

One of the most important activities parents can do is read to their children. Libraries engage children in many ways, helping them learn to love reading. Libraries often have cozy places to sit and read. In one library I visited in San Diego, California, there was a section that looked like a boat, and in another library in Austin, Texas, there was a jungle. Many libraries offer programs for young children during the year and especially during the summer. These can range from studying languages to scavenger hunts. There are also areas for games, puzzles, and computers. Libraries often subscribe to websites and online resources that families can use.

What You Can Do at the Library	
Choose a fun book, and sit with your child and enjoy it.	The act of reading in different locations underscores the joy that reading can bring.
Attend a special event.	For example, LEGO® building, story time, or board game mania.
Invite grandparents to come along.	Make it an intergenerational time by asking grandma or grandpa to read a book to your child.
Share a book with nursery rhymes.	Enjoy the many patterns of language together. One example is *Read-Aloud Rhymes for the Very Young* by Jack Prelutsky and Marc Brown.

Having access to engaging books and oral language experiences is important at this stage in your young child's life. Borrowing books from the library will help teach your child how to take care of the books they borrow and how to keep track of them until it's time to return them.

What You Can Do at Home with Library Books	
Plan quiet time every day to enjoy your child's books.	After bath or just before bedtime work well.
Spend family time together as each person reads their own book.	Demonstrating that you enjoy reading is just as important as reading to your child.
Sit with your child, and share a short book.	*My Mom* by Anthony Browne is a favorite.
While reading, encourage your child act out the story.	A fun book for this is *Jump, Frog, Jump* by Robert Kalan.
Read fiction books.	These help your child enjoy and learn about make-believe. Examples: *Mrs. Wishy-Washy* by Joy Cowley and *Honey . . . Honey . . . Lion!* by Jan Brett.
Read nonfiction books.	These help your child learn more about the world around them. Examples: *ABC Oceans* by the American Museum of Natural History and *Bread, Bread, Bread* by Ann Morris.

Enjoy the library experience with your family, and help your child build memories that will last a lifetime!

A Love for Reading and Learning

by Alexia, Attorney

Looking back, I seem to recollect always loving to read and learn. I think the farthest back I can remember is receiving *Highlights* magazines that we got in the mail. I used to love reading the short stories and doing the activities. One time, I was able to follow the instructions and make a homemade piñata out of a balloon, glue, newspaper, and construction paper. I was so proud of myself!

I eventually graduated to a set of children's encyclopedias that my parents had. I loved the different colors of the covers and using the books to help with my school projects in elementary school. We also had a small bookshelf full of different books. There was never a shortage of reading material!

But my favorite memories come from summers in elementary school. I was able to spend time at the University of Texas at Austin campus with my parents, primarily my mother, who was working toward her Ph.D. She would take us all around campus, to the turtle pond, swim lessons, tennis lessons, the classroom buildings, and the big student library. I felt so grown up going into the library with her and my siblings, as if I were a student. It was so exciting to pick out books to read and sit in the library to read them. There were so many!

As we played video games or read books in the one-bedroom apartment during the summers at the University of Texas, my mother would listen to her recorded lectures and rewrite her notes. I watched her all those years, going to classes, raising kids, and working hard. I knew that I wanted to be able to do that, too.

Now, as I write this, I'm sitting in a public library writing an 8,000-word essay for a class that's part of my LL.M. in International and Comparative Law program. I've completed college and law degrees, but I'm not done. I still love reading and learning—and that came from the beginning.

When I was little, I saw the doors that could be opened and the joy that one gets through learning. Although I don't have my three children with me now as I study in the library, I have brought them to the library and had them work on the computers or read books while I read and study for my classes. It brings back fond memories, and I hope it instills in them a love for learning and reading, just as my experiences did for me.

The Building Blocks to Literacy

Books are sometimes windows, offering views of worlds that may be real or imagined, familiar or strange.

—Dr. Rudine Sims Bishop

Developing a love of reading is so important, and parents can play a crucial role in helping children become successful readers, especially through development of oral vocabulary. Even before they come to school, children and infants soak up words, rhymes, songs, and images. Vocabulary development is particularly important.

Life is so exciting for young children! Everything around them is a new wonder to explore, a learning experience filled with language. You can take advantage of your child's natural curiosity and imagination to create delightful language-learning opportunities that are immersed in play. As children engage with the world around them, literacy can be linked to their experiences. This is especially powerful when parents focus on the building blocks to literacy, beginning as soon as a child is born and continuing through their school career.

What are these building blocks to literacy?

- General oral vocabulary development
- Development of specific oral vocabulary, related to school subjects
- Motivation to read
- Recognition of the individual sounds, or phonemes, in words (phonemic awareness)
- Awareness of other aspects of the sound of language, such as syllables, rhymes, and sentence sound patterns
- Knowing the names of the letters of the alphabet

- Comprehension of stories that are read aloud
- Concepts of print, such as the left to right order of words, the relation of text to pictures, and the idea that letters and combinations of letters represent sounds
- Early attempts at reading
- Early attempts at writing

The following are some ways you can develop these building blocks to literacy at home.

Building Block	Parent Tips
Developing oral vocabulary	This is easy: Talk to your child—a lot! For example, when your child is playing with blocks, bubbles, or toys, use words that describe their shape, color, sound, texture, and other things they can be compared to. Use complete sentences, and ask questions. Everything you do with your child each day is an opportunity to build vocabulary!
Developing school subject vocabulary	School subjects such as reading, math, science, social studies, art, and music have their own sets of vocabulary words. As children play and explore, look for opportunities to talk about what they're doing, using words such as *letter, word, syllable, sentence, rhyme, character, setting, number, more than, less than, add, subtract, community, city, county, world, seed, flower, stem, root, insect, mammal, reptile, color, shade, melody,* and so on.
Motivation to read	The best way to increase your child's motivation to read is simply to read to and with them. And these reading experiences should be enjoyed by both of you! Whether your child is looking through a picture board book, an adult is reading to your child, or your child is reading to an adult, the words, illustrations, characters, and story lines should be celebrated. And be sure to take your child to the library and help them select books.

Building Block	Parent Tips
Recognition of the individual sounds, or phonemes, in words	Think about the words *cat*, *cot*, and *cut*. The sound in the middle has changed, while the beginning and ending sounds have not. Children should learn to recognize such differences not only in the middle of a word but also the beginning of a word (*cat*, *fat*, *mat*, *rat*) or the ending (*cap*, *cat*, *cab*, *can*). One way to develop this ability is to play a "make a word" game while you wait for an appointment, cook dinner, or fold laundry. (Can you change one sound in the word *cat* to make a new word?) Remember, this is about sounds, not letters, so don't write the words.
Awareness of other aspects of the sound of language, such as syllables, rhymes, and sentence sound patterns	There's nothing more powerful than listening to and singing children's songs with your child to develop the awareness of language sounds such as rhymes, syllables, and rhythm. Once your child is familiar with a song or poem, try singing or saying part of it and leaving out the last word. For example, Jack and Jill went up the _____ (*hill*).
Knowing the names of the letters of the alphabet	Place alphabet magnets on your refrigerator or on a baking tray for your child to play with and manipulate. As your child gets older, they can learn to put together the letters in their name. As you drive, point out letters and the way words are put together in traffic signs or in the names of businesses. (This is called *environmental print*.)
Comprehension of stories that are read aloud	When you read aloud, your child should be able to follow along and understand the story. You can help by asking questions about what's happening. The first time, read the book all the way through. After you finish, you can ask questions, such as *What was the story about? Who was in the story? Was it a person or an animal? What happened at the end? How would you change the story? What happened first, second, third, and last in the story? Where did the story take place? What was your favorite part of the story?* On subsequent readings, you can ask questions and talk about what's happening in the story as you read it.

Building Block	Parent Tips
Understanding how books work, such as reading left to right, the order of words, relation of text to pictures, and the idea that letters represent sounds	It's important to help your child understand the parts of books: covers, spine, title page, letters, words, sentences, and illustrations. So, as you read to and with your child, point these out from time to time. Reading Rockets has a Concepts of Print Assessment that's free and easily accessed through a search on their website. It's a useful guide to the kinds of questions you might ask as you enjoy books together.
Early attempts at reading	After you read to and with your child for a while, they will often begin to try to "read" books on their own, mimicking what you've read aloud many times. These are important first steps to reading and should be supported. As you read more books, your child will begin to find words that reappear often in many books. These are called *high-frequency words*. You can support the reading of high-frequency words by labeling a chair, toy box, bed, door, sink, tub, stove, table, or anything your child will enjoy finding and reading. Change them from time to time, and your child will learn to read many new words.
Early attempts at writing	As with reading, it's easy to support your child's writing development in your home. Place writing tools in a shoebox with old envelopes, index cards, leftover printing paper, or little notebooks. This will encourage your child to start the early stages of writing—which include scribbling, drawing, and beginning letter formation—and then progress to labels, words, and more advanced writing. Encourage your child to enjoy the writing process. As I mentioned in a previous chapter, you can even use a brush dipped in a small container of water to "write" on the sidewalk on a hot day. As the writing evaporates, new writing can begin!

The list of ideas for helping your child develop these building blocks to reading can be as vast as your imagination. But here's one more: set a good example by showing your child that you enjoy reading your own books and magazines. And whatever you do to develop literacy with your child, make it joyful—that's how you foster a love of reading that will last a lifetime.

The Power of Stories

by Revital, Senior Curriculum Specialist

My grandparents taught me to appreciate the intellectual capacity of children. I vividly remember sitting on my grandmother's living room floor when I was about eight years old, listening to her read Shakespeare's *The Taming of the Shrew* and Poe's "The Tell-Tale Heart." My grandparents had a set of children's versions of classic stories, which they must have purchased for the purpose of reading to my brother and me. Looking back, I realize that I had no idea what was happening in the stories, but it didn't matter. I loved to listen to them. The books were leather-bound and thick. They were about romance and death and darkness— things I didn't normally get to hear about. Whenever we visited, I would beg to hear the stories from those books.

My grandparents did not have college degrees or fancy jobs, but they were European and loved the arts. My grandfather was a Hungarian immigrant who worked as the foreman of a steel mill in Detroit for his entire life, but he also spoke eight languages and played the oboe. My grandmother, the daughter of Hungarian immigrants, raised three children and worked at the food co-op, where they bought all their food, and she sewed costumes for their local folk-dance troupe. When they passed away, they left us with dozens of instruments, embroideries, cookbooks, costumes, and lots of books.

I appreciate so much that they chose to read us "real literature" instead of whatever my friends were reading at the time. When I became a teacher, I centered my reading program around long multichapter read-alouds and quality literature. There is nothing more magical than the hush that falls over a room of children when you pull out a book and open to the bookmarked chapter, or when they'd rather hear another chapter than go outside for recess, or when they start a sign-up sheet to take the book home after you finish the last chapter. My grandparents taught me the power of literature, and I have done my best to pass that lesson on. I am forever grateful to them.

Learning to Count and Counting on Learning

If I were again beginning my studies, I would follow the advice of Plato and start with mathematics.

—Galileo Galilei

One of the first learning experiences to provide for your young child is counting because it's a complex experience and an important building block for understanding the concepts of numbers and mathematics.

Usually, the first counting-related skill that children learn is the ability to recite the words for the numbers in the correct order: *one, two, three, four, five*. . . . This memory skill is important (just as it is useful to know "The Alphabet Song" to learn the names and order of the letters of the alphabet), yet even as children begin to recite the numbers in order, they typically don't have any understanding of what the words *one, two, three,* and so forth actually mean. According to the National Council of Teachers of Mathematics, the standard for numbers and operations for prekindergarten through grade 2 is "count with understanding and recognize 'how many' in sets of objects." When children "count with understanding," they understand that the word *one* refers to one object of any kind, the word *two* refers to two objects, and so on.

Everyday experiences can lead children to discover and understand the relationship between quantities and the words that are used to talk about numbers. For example, when counting, children need to learn that there is a one-to-one correspondence of object and number (like matching one person to one cookie) and that counting two after one means that the first and second objects need to be added together to make two, and so on!

When you give your child things to count, start with the objects displayed in a line so they can see each object individually and count the objects sequentially:

 (10)

Counting from left to right and touching each object as it is counted helps your child understand the one-to-one correspondence of an object to a number. In addition, moving objects closer together while they count will help your child understand that the number *four*, for instance, refers to all the objects counted up to four and not just the one called *four*:

You can also provide practice in recognizing sets of objects by the way they are grouped, such as the dots on a six-sided number cube. Children can count the dots, recognize the pattern, and learn that they won't have to count again as the set/pattern becomes associated with the quantity it represents. The following simple game can help:

1. Hold five or six small objects (buttons, grapes, pennies) in your hand.

2. Roll a different number of them.

3. Tell your child to look at the objects you rolled and quickly name the quantity without counting.

4. Repeat this activity.

After a while, your child will be able to quickly identify and tell the number for each quantity of objects.

Additionally, provide practice in recognizing sets of objects by the way they are grouped in a line, like this:

The most important thing about teaching counting and other early mathematics concepts to your child is that they should see numbers as part of their real-life experiences. Look for opportunities to count with your child whenever possible. For example, you might count everyday items, such as these:

- packages of macaroni or beans in the kitchen
- leaves that have fallen from a tree
- buttons on a jacket or sweater
- school buses you see on the drive to school
- forks, spoons, knives, plates, and napkins to match the total number of people eating together

To nurture your child's grasp of numbers and counting, continue to ask them questions such as these:

- How many shells did you find? Please count them one by one to find out.

- Did you look at all the petals on this flower? Please count them to find out how many petals there are in all.

- See these two beans? Let's add two more beans. Please put them together and count them to find out how many beans you have in all.

Integrating counting into your child's life will help them understand that counting is an essential skill that's important to learn—like learning to read.

Here are a few captivating children's books that will help your child develop the concept of counting:
- *Doggies* by Sandra Boynton
- *1-2-3: A Child's First Counting Book* by Alison Jay
- *Roar! A Noisy Counting Book* by Pamela Duncan Edwards
- *Miss Spider's Tea Party: The Counting Book* by David Kirk
- *Ten Little Ladybugs* by Melanie Gerth
- *One Fox: A Counting Book Thriller* by Kate Read
- *Count the Dinosaurs* by Books for Little Ones
- *1, 2, 3, Animals! A First Counting Book for Toddlers* by Bethany Lake

The time you spend with your child on this subject will help when they encounter numbers—in preschool, pre-k, or kindergarten—and they will already understand that these symbols and words represent quantities. Mathematics educators call this *understanding*, and it's an essential foundation for your child's future mathematics learning.

The key foundation skill of counting and the concept of quantity will help your child develop an awareness about numbers that will serve them forever. This is vital because your youngster can count on counting being around for their whole life!

Counting Memories

by Phyllis, Editor

My father died when I was two, and we went to live with my grandparents. Three years later, my grandfather passed away. So, I was raised and taught by my mother and my grandmother—two loving, resilient, and hard-working women.

Early on, my mother was a high school English teacher; then, she became the editor of a magazine comprised of students' articles related to the history of Illinois. My grandmother, who was in her seventies, took on the daytime responsibilities of caring for my older brother and me.

On my first day of kindergarten, Mom gave me a bag with my own pencils, ruler, erasers, and 20 empty thread spools for counting. But I soon discovered that everyone else had painted thread spools; I was sad and envious. When I finally told Mom many weeks later, she secretly began painting another set of spools. She presented them to me after the gifts were opened on Christmas morning. I was amazed, and I still remember how happy and proud I felt as I showed them to my classmates! The new spools were so bright and shiny that I can still see them in my mind's eye.

Meanwhile, after my grandmother learned that I was the only child without painted spools, she dumped out four of her huge jars of beautiful buttons into two shoeboxes. Then, she told me that I could pick 20 of them—once I could count that high. I remember it took days to find my favorite ones, but it took longer to count them. My grandmother practiced with me all the time. We counted everything: rocks, sidewalk cracks, trees, flowers, sticks, caterpillars, clouds, leaves, and birds—anything she could find nearby. As we took our walks together, hand in hand, she was helping me learn, not only how to count but also how beautiful our world is! I know now that it was extremely hard for her to walk because she had crippling arthritis. Regardless, we walked every day, mostly around our yard, but we always walked and counted together. On rainy days, besides buttons, we counted her teacup collection; bobby pins; spoons; her sparkly jewelry; tubes of lipstick; pennies; skeins of colorful, soft yarn; bottles in the refrigerator; and best of all, her homemade star-shaped shortbread cookies.

Within about two weeks, I reached my goal of 20; soon, I reached 30, and eventually 100! Sixty years later, I still smile remembering the day that I brought in my own jar of 100 special buttons to school. I was very proud. Next thing I knew, my classmates were trying to count that high to get their own buttons!

Today, I am an editor and writer, and I love how words "fit" together. Math doesn't always come easy for me, but I learned early on to keep at it, no matter how long it takes. These are gifts from two incredible, inspirational women!

Children Making Sense of Numbers: Number Sense

Number sense is one of the most difficult concepts to teach young children. Why? Because it's abstract.

For children to grasp number sense, they need to understand that an abstract symbol (the numeral *3* or *8*, for example) means an amount or quantity that could apply to anything. They need to learn that the numeral *7* can stand for the number of girls in the room, cups in a box, blocks on a table, pieces of a puzzle, or scrapes they have on their legs. And they need to learn that a *6* means less than a *9*, even though there's no way to understand that just by looking at the numerals themselves. But once children develop number sense, wow!—their math abilities can really take off!

Young learners love knowing that numbers can represent everything from a little pebble in the palm of their hand to the billions of grains of sand on a beach. For curious children and those who truly understand what numbers and their symbols represent, numbers are like magic!

To teach number sense, begin with the numbers *1* to *10* because we use a base-ten system, and these are the numbers that young learners are most familiar with. Try to give your child as many oral- and visual-counting experiences as possible during their first five years.

The following chart shows simple activities that can help your child develop number sense.

Activity	Parent Tips
Count out loud with your child whenever possible so they hear numbers frequently and learn to associate them with objects in the world.	For example, you might say, "How many toes are on your foot? One, two, three, four, five. Five toes!" Or you might say, "How many socks are in your drawer? Let's count them!"
Help your child learn that the quantities you are counting can be written with a symbol, called a *numeral*.	You might say, "Now that you can count to 10, let me show you how you can write the numbers that you count! *1 2 3 4 5 6 7 8 9 10*."
Talk about what numbers mean to you and how you use them.	Explain how you use numbers to measure ingredients in a recipe or measure how tall your child is; to count your money; to tell time; to pay bills; to use the numbers on a telephone, a TV remote, and a computer keyboard; and to identify your street address.
Help your child see math in their everyday world.	You might say something like, "When you counted all these letters that we got in the mail today, you counted six of them. We can write that like this: *6*. And if we received one more letter, we would have seven, which is the next number after 6. One, two, three, four, five, six . . . seven."
Compare numbers.	Count small crackers or pretzels and place them into groups of different sizes to help your child to see the difference. For example, you could point out that a group of two stacked crackers is smaller than a group of five stacked crackers. Or count blocks as you stack them. Then, show that a stack of six blocks is much taller than a stack of three blocks.

Activity	Parent Tips
Place magnetic numbers on your refrigerator or a metal baking pan.	Move the numbers to a place next to the things your child counts while you are cooking.
As your child is learning to count to 20, talk about how the pattern of numbers is different after number 10.	Explain that some of the numbers, such as 11, 12, 13, and 15, don't sound like the numbers your child is familiar with. (This makes 11 through 20 the hardest group of numbers for children to learn.)
Indicate that once your child counts beyond 10, they will count using tens and ones.	Explain that 20 means two 10s and zero 1s; 21 means two 10s and one 1, 22 means two 10s and two 1s, and so on.
Play with dominoes.	Have your child match the number patterns on the dominoes. Have them count how many fives are in the set of dominoes. Count with your child to show how two of the 5s equal 10.
Make a numbers chart on a large piece of posterboard.	Start by writing 1–10 across the top. After a few weeks of working with your child, add 11–20 in the next row, creating columns, then 21–30, and eventually over weeks and months, build up the chart to 100.
Use the numbers chart to gradually introduce addition.	For example, point to the number 2, and then count two more on the chart to show $2 + 2 = 4$.

You can also read books about numbers and number sense to your child.

- *The Icky Bug Counting Book* by Jerry Pallotta
- *10 Little Rubber Ducks* by Eric Carle
- *Centipede's 100 Shoes* by Tony Ross
- *Fall Is Here! Counting 1 to 10* by Pamela Jane
- *Big Book of Counting to 100: Find, Discover, Learn* by Ekaterina Ladatko
- *When I Am Big (A Counting Book from 1 to 25)* by Maria Dek
- *Not Just Another Counting Book: A Book for Clever Counters* by Kay Mon Rey

Numbers are sometimes intimidating to children. But by introducing math concepts early and showing how numbers are a part of your world, you'll help your child to develop number sense early. You'll also help them enjoy math more because your youngster is learning it with you!

Math with Dad

by Marshall, High School Teacher

Throughout my childhood, my dad was always the uncomplicated and reserved parent. He would go to work, come home, help make dinner with my mother, and then he was off to bed. My mother would always be the one to help my siblings and me with our homework assignments.

But one evening, I was working on an extra-credit math problem for my sixth grade math class. As a student, I was very good at math, but I was dismayed by the level of difficulty of the math problem. My dad noticed me struggling with the problem, and he offered to help. To my astonishment, he was able to solve the problem within a minute.

After asking my dad about the steps for solving the problem, I learned that he'd loved math as a child. He was even a member of his school's math club. My dad rarely discussed his life as a child, so having him talk to me about his childhood was exciting. Up until that moment, I had no idea about my dad's interest in math.

After that pivotal evening, I began asking my dad for help with all my math homework. I was happy to have my dad tutor me in math, and I could tell he was happy to help me.

I later learned that if he'd been given the opportunity, my dad would've wanted to study engineering or physics in college. Knowing that my dad never had the chance to attend college, I was determined to work hard in high school so I could attend college and make him proud. I'm happy to say that I became the first male from his side of the family to graduate from college. Thanks to my dad's guidance, I'm now a high school teacher, and I help students learn—just as my father helped me.

Science: Setting the Stage

Libraries and museums are powerful but
often overlooked partners in learning.
—Campaign for Grade-Level Reading

Science museums have amazing exhibits where children can creatively and happily explore topics in engaging ways. But learning about science doesn't need to be limited to a museum. Create a discovery zone in your own home to help your child explore topics of interest.

1. Find out what your child is most interested in. Is it bugs or bubbles? How about shadows and light or sound and vibrations? Perhaps it's things that move or things that grow? One great way to find out is to visit a library or secondhand bookstore and find the section that has science books for young readers of your child's age. Place several of them on a table, and see what book(s) your child chooses.

2. Bring some of those books home, and read them together to set the stage.

3. Look around for things in your house, at the market, or online that will help your child explore and spur their interest in the topic. If the topic is light and shadows, for example, the equipment and materials might include flashlights, mirrors, cardboard, safety scissors, and colored cellophane.

4. Set up the equipment and materials in a specially designated "exploration zone" for a week or so, depending on your child's interest. With young children, it's always a good idea to allow exploration to occur in a series of relatively brief sessions over a span of time.

5. Take some photographs as your child experiments with the materials. Many children at this stage are so immersed in their work that they may not want to communicate or answer questions right then, but when they see the photos later, they'll have much to say! If your child does want to talk while exploring, ask questions, such as "Why does it look like that?" or "What can you do to make it grow?" You can also think of other thought-provoking questions. These will help develop critical thinking and problem-solving skills.

6. Once your child has finished the activity, present the pictures you took and ask them what was happening and what they found out. This review is important in developing your child's recognition of sequences of events and language skills.

7. If you can, print the pictures, glue them into a small journal or book, and have your child dictate a story (for you to write) about what was happening in the photograph(s). This way, you are showing them that ideas can be written, which is an important literacy concept for young children.

Problem-Solving

by Michelle, Senior Graphic Design Manager

I come from a family with many, many teachers. I was also the first grandchild on both sides of my family, so I had a lot of time with grown-ups to explore and ask questions— so very many questions! When I wore one adult out, they would send me to ask another adult. Thankfully, there was always someone who loved me that was ready to explain whatever I was fixated on at that moment in a new way.

My dad is not a teacher by trade but an engineer, and he LOVES explaining things. So, when Dad was home, Mom would joyfully send me his way. I would follow him around as he moved from one project around the house to another, and I was relentless: "Why are these pliers pointy? Why is the drywall chalky? Why should I not touch the insulation? Why does the attic smell different?" He always had an amazingly complicated answer that he would break down for me, and I was able to get it.

I remember one weekend, not long after I had learned how to ride a two-wheel bike. I discovered that my tire was flat. My dad and I sat on the front stoop with my bike, a patch kit, a wrench, and a bucket. While we took apart my tire, we talked about the different parts. After we discussed how each part contributed to a working tire, he asked me where I thought the problem was. We quickly connected the dots between the tube in my bike tire and an inflatable raft at the pool, and I suggested that there might be a hole somewhere. Then, he asked, "Well, how can we find it?" So, we filled the bucket with water, and he showed me how to test each section of the tube. He left me with it for a while, and eventually, I found the leak. He then showed me how to clean the surface, apply a patch, assemble the tire, fill the tire, and test the pressure so I could ride my bike again.

My dad taught me how to identify problems practically and find solutions. Today, it's one of my favorite things about being a parent. Whenever I watch my kids dissect a problem or question and find a solution, I think of that bike tire tube in a bucket of water—and my dad.

Science Explorations

Children love hands-on science. They're eager
to learn and see how the world works.

—Nancy Young

In the previous chapter, I wrote about science and ways to set the stage for science explorations. My first suggestion was to find out about your child's interests and set up an experience or exploration with that in mind. I asked, "Is your child interested in bugs or bubbles? How about shadows and light or sound and vibrations? Perhaps it's things that move or things that grow."

Here are some suggestions for setting up exploration "zones" with those themes.

Insects

As with anything, safety comes first, so when dealing with insects and young children, it's important to always have an adult present to keep the youngster safe.

Activities

Set up a small area in your home for insect observing. You'll need a jar with holes in the lid so that your child can observe the insects for a day or two before releasing them.

Dollar stores sell nets and containers for observing insects, and some pet stores sell crickets that you can purchase inexpensively to observe and then release. You can also purchase an ant farm, which usually comes with a coupon to populate the farm.

I have also captured ants from my backyard and placed them in my ant farm. I released them after about two weeks, but by then they had already dug complex and fascinating pattern tunnels in the perlite sand.

You can try to use a net to capture a butterfly in your backyard as well. Sometimes, just lying on a blanket on the grass can help you find insects deep in the grass.

If you don't have a yard, go to a park or take a nature walk to look for some insects.

Questions

- What are some different kinds of insects?
- How are insects the same? How are they different?
- What colors are insects?
- What do insects need to live?

Books

- *Are You an Ant?* by Judy Allen
- *The Backyard Bug Book for Kids: Storybook, Insect Facts, and Activities* by Lauren Davidson
- *Insects & Bugs for Kids: An Introduction to Entomology* by Jaret C. Daniels
- The following titles by Cheryl Coughlan: *Beetles, Bumble Bees, Crickets, Dragonflies, Fireflies, Grasshoppers, Ladybugs, Mosquitoes*

Shadows and Light

It's fun to play with shadows and light, whether in the sun outdoors or with a flashlight indoors. Set up an indoor area where you can keep your flashlights and other objects, such as small stuffed animals and small plastic toys. Read several books about shadows with your child to help them understand the properties of light.

Activities

Hold up an object, such as a stuffed toy, or place it on a flat surface. Have your child hold a flashlight in front of it, and then move the flashlight closer or farther away. Discuss the changes in the shadow.

Go outside during the morning and observe the shadow of a tree. Then, go outside at noon, in the afternoon, and in the evening, and compare the locations of the shadows. Discuss how the changes happened.

Have your child "play" with their shadow, making it move as your child moves into different positions.

Questions

- What is outdoors that can make shadows?
- Can you make a shadow outdoors? How did you do it?
- How can we make shadows indoors?
- Can you make the shadow bigger? How?
- Can you make the shadow smaller? How?

Books

- *Day Light, Night Light: Where Light Comes From* by Franklyn M. Branley
- *Moonbear's Shadow* by Frank Asch
- *Shadows and Reflections* by Tana Hoban
- *What Makes Day and Night* by Franklyn M. Branley
- *Whoo's There? A Bedtime Shadow Book* by Heather Zschock
- *I See a Shadow* by Laura Breen
- *My Shadow* by Robert Louis Stevenson and Sara Sanchez

Sound and Vibration

If you don't mind noise, this will be a fun exploration! Almost anything can make sound, and you can control the volume by choosing the materials that your child plays with.

Activities

Place small pots and pans with some wooden spoons in your child's exploration area, and encourage them to have at it.

Place a variety of objects that make noise in a basket: a rattle, two spoons, a well-sealed container partially filled with macaroni or beans, rhythm sticks, a maraca, or any rhythm instrument.

Use three or more small water glasses with different levels of water in them. Tap the glasses with a pencil, and listen to the sounds. Compare the different levels of water with the different pitches of sound.

Cut a long piece of string, and have your child hold one end while you hold the other. Pull it tight, pluck the string, and have your child feel the vibration on the string.

Questions

- What are some different kinds of sounds?
- What can you use to make different sounds?
- How can you make sounds loud and soft?
- How can you make sounds high and low?

Books

- *All about Sound* by Lisa Trumbauer
- *Polar Bear, Polar Bear, What Do You Hear?* by Bill Martin Jr. and Eric Carle
- *The Sense of Hearing* by Elaine Landau
- *Sound: Loud, Soft, High, and Low* by Natalie M. Rosinsky
- *Sounds All Around: The Science of How Sound Works* by Susan Hughes
- *Sounds All Around* by Wendy Pfeffer and Anna Chernyshova
- *Sound* by Romana Romanyshyn and Andriy Lesiv

The Ants Go Marching . . .

by Adelfino, Operations Manager

"Fino, don't pick up the big red ones!" That quote stands out in my mind from when we were searching for ants to build our very own ant farm. The big red ones were fire ants, and they would have bitten me. Growing up, we were fortunate enough to live next to a park where there was an abundance of small animals and insects. My mother would often have us go collect insects so we could learn about them while having fun. We learned about how ants build tunnels and how they live and work in their colonies.

When I think back on my childhood, those are some of the most cherished moments I have with my sisters and parents. Now, I have young children of my own. My wife and I try to keep them active and teach them while having fun. This past summer, we wanted to hike a trail, which was a new experience. I thought back to the times when I would collect insects, so we bought necklace bug jars for each child. During the hike, we caught all kinds of insects, but mostly butterflies. We talked about the life cycle of the butterfly so we could have fun and learn.

The experiences I was able to share with my family when I was young left a lasting impression that I'm now passing on to my kids. I hope they will do the same!

More Science Explorations

*In every walk with nature, one receives
far more than he seeks.*

—John Muir

When it comes to explorations based on science activities, there is always more for your child to discover. This chapter offers some activities to try with wheels, balls, and motion, and with seeds and plants.

Wheels, Balls, and Motion

Motion is fascinating for young children. They love to throw, roll, catch, and watch things move. You can either create an indoor space or an outdoor space for this exploration.

Activities

Gather all the wheeled toys, such as small cars or planes, you can find around the house, and place them in a basket or plastic tub. Set up ramps to give your child the opportunity to roll the small cars down the ramps. Then, change the angle of each ramp as an exploration. Once your child has had a week or two to experiment with the vehicles, you can place balls, such as golf balls or ping pong balls, in the bin to roll. Try including small square blocks for comparison.

You and your child can also gather various things that will roll: a curler, a rolling pin, a pencil, a plastic bottle or jar, an apple, or different kinds of balls, hoops, or cylinders. You can also create an outdoor exploration area where your child can try rolling, throwing, kicking, and moving things in different ways.

Questions

- Where can you find wheels in the house or outside?
- How can you make something move faster on a ramp?
- How much faster can you make something go?
- How can you slow something down?
- What things roll the best?

Books
- *Big Wheels* by Anne Rockwell
- *Rolling* by Sara E. Hoffmann
- *What Do Wheels Do All Day?* by April Jones Prince
- *What Is a Wheel and Axle?* by Lloyd G. Douglas
- *Wheels on the Go!* by La Coccinella
- *Wheels and Axles* by Martha Elizabeth Hillman Rustad
- *Simple Machines* by D. J. Ward and Mike Lowery

Seeds and Plants

Seeds and plants are one of my favorite explorations because they're everywhere and are easy to obtain. Young children can learn that plants come from seeds; that seeds come in various sizes, shapes, and colors; and that plants need water, soil, air, and light to live.

Activities

Create an exploration area in your kitchen where you and your child can look at dry seeds, such as pinto, lima, or navy beans. Ask your child to sort them by color or size.

When you're cooking, save the seeds from inside vegetables or fruits for your child to look at through a hand lens, or small magnifying glass. Compare the size of a strawberry seed (which is one of the few seeds that grows on the outside of a fruit) to the size of a watermelon seed.

Help your child plant the seeds in small cups, planters, or other containers that have a small hole in the bottom.

One of my favorite school activities is to place a moistened paper towel in a small plastic bag and place four bean seeds in it. Place the baggie in a sunny area and the seeds should germinate in two to three days! Experiment with other dry seeds or with those that you found in the fruits and vegetables. Talk about what's happening with the seeds.

If you have space outside, your child can plant seeds in a small area or planter to create an outdoor garden. Explain why it's important to water the plants and how they require air and light.

Questions

- What is a seed?
- How are seeds similar to and different from each other?
- What seeds do you want to plant? Why?
- What are some parts of a plant?
- What do plants need to live?
- What do leaves/roots/stems do?
- What do roots do?
- What do stems do?

Books
- *From Seed to Plant* by Allan Fowler
- *From Seed to Plant* by Gail Gibbons
- *Seeds* by Vijaya Khisty Bodach
- *Seed, Soil, Sun: Earth's Recipe for Food* by Cris Peterson
- *Seeds Go, Seeds Grow* by Mark Weakland
- *The Tiny Seed* by Eric Carle
- *The Amazing Life Cycle of Plants* by Kay Barnharn
- *My First Book of House Plants* by Duopress Labs
- *Plant the Tiny Seed* by Christie Matheson

Whether it's a museum, the forest, a park, the beach, your backyard, your kitchen, or books from the library, you can create a wonder-filled summer of exploration if you think of everything in your environment as an opportunity to teach science to your child.

My Reading Heritage

by Eduardo, Spanish Language Specialist

I have a love for reading that started when I was a child, and for that, I have my two grandfathers to thank. One of my grandfathers was a machinist by trade. I'm not sure how much education he received, but he was kind and liked by everybody. He also played professional baseball in his prime.

My other grandfather was a diesel mechanic, I think. But I believe his first love was farming, something he did for as long as I can remember. He only studied to the sixth grade, yet he was as well-read as my college professors who assisted me with my thesis project. He loved gymnastics and was an extremely fit grandfather.

Both were named Francisco.

As a child, I would often visit my grandfather that was the baseball player, and one of the reasons was that he would buy comic books for me to read. Before I knew that Tarzan was a character made up by a European writer, I was reading about him and his exploits in the jungle, with the comics. I even learned and often performed the manly and wild scream that Tarzan would do, right from the front porch of my grandparents' house. Through the comics, I also grew to know Disney characters as well as superheroes. My favorites were Batman, Green Arrow, and Aquaman. I didn't care much for Superman.

My other grandpa, the farmer, would read books like *20,000 Leagues Under the Sea*, *The Three Musketeers*, *White Fang*, and *The Count of Monte Cristo*, among others, aloud to me. I don't think I ever finished the books with him. I wasn't patient enough to stick around to finish any of those novels in one sitting (and certainly not *Crime and Punishment*, which I still haven't read). He also read me the poetry of Amado Nervo, Neruda, Bécquer, and Darío. While I only mostly understood the patriotic poetry and simple verses, I frequently competed in declamation contests and often won.

Both of my grandfathers passed away many years ago, yet today in my collection of literary works, you'll find a few of the classics—many of them in the form of comics or illustrated novels.

¡Gracias, queridos abuelos!

The Wonder of Weather for Children

I am among those who think that science
has great beauty. A scientist in his
laboratory is not only a technician: he is also
a child placed before natural phenomena
which impress him like a fairy tale.

—Marie Curie

Natural phenomena are fascinating to young children. Thunder, lightning, rainbows, bugs crawling, leaves falling, a bird building a nest, and water flowing after a heavy rainstorm are all intriguing to observe.

Over time, there have been severe tropical storms and hurricanes that have dominated the news. Most children have heard about such (sometimes scary) storms, so it's especially important that they learn about the weather and all the changes weather can cause for people and their homes as well as for plants and animals. Such well-publicized weather events are opportunities to build science knowledge and skills. Expect your child to be fully engaged: big weather events have an almost magical fairy-tale appeal and can be both scary and full of wonder for children.

First, families can help their children by calmly talking about how to be prepared for weather emergencies. Making children feel safe is as important as explaining how these weather events happen.

When dramatic weather events occur, it's a good time to help children understand more about where they live in relation to where the events are and to compare what's going on in their neighborhood with what's happening in the Atlantic Ocean, Pacific Ocean, the Caribbean, or the Gulf of Mexico. You can discuss which areas are most likely to experience different types of severe weather and why.

Studying the weather can include many aspects of science:

- sunlight
- air and wind
- temperature
- rain, snow, sleet, hail, fog, and drizzle
- water
- clouds
- shadows
- weather changes
- seasonal changes

There are also many wonderful books on these topics:

- *Weather Forecasting* by Gail Gibbons
- *A Place Where Hurricanes Happen* by Shadra Strickland
- *Water Is Water: A Book About the Water Cycle* by Miranda Paul
- *Pop! Air and Water Pressure* by Stephanie Paris
- *When the Sky Breaks: Hurricanes, Tornadoes, and the Worst Weather in the World* by Simon Winchester
- *What Will the Weather Be?* by Lynda DeWitt
- *Down Comes the Rain* by Franklyn M. Branley
- *What Is Severe Weather?* by Jennifer Boothroyd

After reading about weather, consider starting a family project to observe the weather around you for a week or a month, and document your observations in a journal. Children can draw pictures for the journal and either write about their pictures or get help from an adult to write their thoughts.

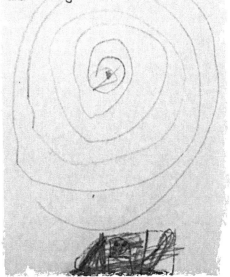

The calm part is in the middle, and the big circles are not calm. They suck up the water and then it goes into people's houses.

To the right is a picture that one of my grandchildren drew after we evacuated for Hurricane Harvey. She dictated her thoughts about the picture, and her mother wrote them for her. You can also see where she drew herself inside the house. This kind of activity gives children a way to be part of the conversation and to express their ideas and fears when the adults around them are talking about weather events.

Because water plays such a large role in weather events, another suggestion is for you and your child to do activities that focus on water and its properties.

The following are some activities to try with water:

- Freeze it, melt it, pour it, and watch it evaporate over time.
- Float or sink things in it using a small bowl or bin.
- Come up with and discuss water-related words, such as *splashing, falling, dripping, drizzling, raining,* and *wetting.*

As your child learns about the weather through activities such as these, they will also develop an academic vocabulary (nouns, verbs, adjectives, and adverbs) that enables them to understand and express more complex ideas on many topics.

The wonder of weather is that every day is a new learning opportunity!

When Mother Nature Has a Mind of Her Own

by Catherine, Staff Writer

When I was seven years old, I woke up in the dark of night to my bedroom vigorously shaking. I immediately ran to my parents' bedroom, and they calmly held me, reassuring me that things would be fine. When the shaking stopped, they pulled out an emergency bag they kept under their bed and turned on the coolest yellow flashlight that also happened to be a radio.

Growing up in Southern California, my parents stressed the importance of being prepared for as long as I can remember. Their emergency bag wasn't just for earthquakes—it was for storms, floods, brush fires, and any other situation where Mother Nature had a mind of her own. Both my mother and father believed in preparedness, and they also believed very strongly in knowledge being a powerful force against fear.

I had so many questions about the Earth at that age. When would the ground shake that hard again? Could lightning "get me" while indoors? How likely was it that a tornado would pick up our house, like in *The Wizard of Oz*? After explaining what they could (*no one knows for sure; no;* or *not likely at all*),

they also bought me a book about the Earth. It had colorful pictures, diagrams, and many facts about both geological and meteorological phenomena. I became engrossed in this book! I learned about earthquakes and volcanic eruptions, as well as hurricanes, tornadoes, tsunamis, and more. The more I read about these phenomena, the less I feared them.

I'm incredibly grateful for how my parents approached the unpredictable nature of the Earth. Rather than dismissing my fears or telling me to merely trust the adults, they empowered me with knowledge. Their encouragement of my curiosity and their example of preparedness made me less afraid of Mother Nature. I've carried these lessons with me into adulthood. You better believe I have my own yellow emergency radio/flashlight—and it's just as cool as theirs!

STEAM for Young Learners

The most certain way to succeed is always to try just one more time.

—Thomas Edison

I'm encouraged by initiatives in many schools known as STEAM. These refer to units of study that combine ideas and skills in Science, Technology, Engineering, the Arts, and Mathematics. This idea of interconnecting content enables children to think and play in ways that are creative and bolster their confidence, engagement, and enthusiasm for learning.

STEAM is a philosophy. It is science and technology, interpreted through the actual design of something using engineering and the arts, all described and planned using mathematical elements.

Here's another way to think about STEAM:

- S(cience): a way of thinking
- T(echnology): a way of doing
- E(ngineering): a way of building
- A(rts): a way of creating
- M(athematics): a way of measuring

What's expected of students is to take the ways that we think, do, build, create, and measure, and use them together to be critical and creative thinkers. This means that as parents, you can provide the first foundation for your children's experiences by giving them opportunities to think, do, build, create, and measure.

The following chart shows some examples.

STEAM Topic	Activities
Science	✦ Observe weather. ✦ Observe living things for similarities and differences and patterns of growth. ✦ Explore balance, weight, gravity, motion, and momentum with small toy cars and ramps or on outdoor play structures, such as swings, motion rides, and balance beams. ✦ Notice cause-and-effect relationships in physical and chemical changes, as in cooking and making clay pots.
Technology	✦ Use apps to design and create. ✦ Use digital devices to search for information and to communicate. ✦ Take and manipulate pictures.
Engineering	✦ Create things with blocks or other "open-ended" materials, such as spools, straws, craft sticks, and modeling clay. ✦ Play with construction toys. ✦ Make things with child-friendly household tools and materials, such as cardboard boxes and tubes.
Arts	✦ Work in a variety of media. ✦ Learn about colors and shades of colors. ✦ Use art apps.
Mathematics	✦ Measure and document changes over time. ✦ Sort information. ✦ Create and extend patterns. ✦ Make pictographs and bar graphs.

Launch with a Book

Set the stage for these learning activities by reading a book. There are many wonderful choices. Afterward, talk to your child about what project you could do related to what you read; then, gather the tools and materials needed, create a design, and build! Here are two examples.

If You Find a Rock

This book, by Peggy Christian and Barbara Hirsch Lember, is full of pictures of all kinds of rocks, found in all kinds of places. It will help children appreciate the beauty and surprises in the natural world that surrounds them.

Materials

- rocks
- modeling clay
- paper
- crayons, pencil, markers
- ruler or stacking blocks to determine height

Activity

After reading the book, discuss it with your child and ask them questions, such as:

- Do you think we could make a house out of rocks?
- Why are rocks good for that?
- What kind of house should we make?
- Should we use big rocks or small rocks?
- How can we hold the rocks together?
- What should the house look like?
- How tall should it be?
- How many rocks do you think we'll need?
- Should we try to get rocks of different colors or the same color?
- Where can we find them?

Cuckoo

I mentioned this book previously. *Cuckoo*, by Lois Ehlert, is a Mexican folktale about a bird who's considered vain and doesn't help the other animals with the work of gathering seeds for the winter. When a fire threatens the crop, Cuckoo surprises everyone by helping to save the seeds for food the next year. The book contains geometric illustrations and bright, vivid colors, reminiscent of the art forms of Mexico.

Materials

- tagboard
- many colors of construction paper
- glue
- scissors

Activity

After reading the book, ask your child to help you make a bird. Creating a bird that is three-dimensional includes the engineering component, making it a STEAM activity. Ask questions, such as:

- What parts make up the body of a bird?
- What shapes could you use to make the bird?
- How many shapes do you need to make the bird?
- How can you make the eyes, beak, wings, talons, and body of the bird using simple geometric shapes?
- Can you plan it?
- What colors could you use to distinguish the parts of the bird?
- Can we engineer the bird so it will stand?

STEAM activities are great for weekends or any day when you have some time! Once you've made something, leave it up over time so that your child can build on and add to it or try different designs. Take pictures of your child working on STEAM activities, and write captions for them. You'll not only be using science, technology, engineering, art, and mathematics to create things—you'll also be creating memories!

Music and the Worldwide Family

by Willow, Music Teacher

My father was a musician and my mother a dancer. I used to sleep in my father's guitar case while he performed in the halls of our small country town of Nimbin, Australia. I still want to climb in when I feel the velvet lining of guitar cases today. There was never a social gathering without instruments coming out. I was sung to sleep as my father played his mandolin, and from the age of eight years old, the one thing that would get my father to turn off the TV was inviting him to jam on the blues with me playing harmonica.

My sister and my mother were dancers, and we have four generations of dancers in our maternal line. My grandmother was in the Royal Australian Ballet company.

The music of Prince and old soul records were some of our favorites to dance to, and we would have family "dance-offs" in the living room often. My sister would teach me moves, and as a teen in the '90s, I was doing the running man and the Kid 'n Play—so uncool now.

My mother's musicality was so well honed she would yell out "you're leaving the beat," when I was practicing saxophone with play-along records.

Music and dance were always about celebrating community. I joined a new community of jazz musicians and later traveled the world playing music with people of many cultures and musical genres from Asia all the way to Latin America. I believe music and dance are truly at the root of our humanity and will carry us forward if we cherish and celebrate it. "If you can walk, you can dance; if you can talk, you can sing," goes the African proverb.

Teaching Young Children About Work

Don't judge each day by the harvest you reap but by the seeds that you plant.

—Robert Louis Stevenson

One of the first books that I read to my class at the beginning of every school year was *The Grasshopper and the Ants*, an Aesop's Fable. I believed that it was very important to instill in children early on that work is important and that coming to school is their work.

This story sets the tone for our learning about work: All learners should work like the ants—not sit around and do nothing like the grasshopper. Children are always quick to find fault with the grasshopper, seeing that he wasn't willing to work to collect food for the winter. Great! If they get it, they will be ready to work!

Work is an important part of life. That's one reason why children should learn about the professions and trades that they can observe within or near their own communities: firefighters, teachers, police officers, mail carriers, doctors, nurses, farmers, cooks, retailers, builders, and so many others. It's also important that children learn about jobs people have that they may not see, such as computer programmers, graphic designers, wildlife biologists, and so on.

Here are a few suggestions for helping your child understand the importance of work and people doing their work.

Suggestions	Tips and Examples
Talk about your work and the work done by other members of the family.	As a teacher, I was surprised to find that many young children said that their mom or dad went to work but didn't know what that meant or what their work was.
Discuss with your child the jobs that you encounter as you go about your day.	At the grocery store, talk about the bakers, the dairy farmers, the produce farmers, and the cashiers. When driving, point out the police officers, firefighters, and gardeners. When you see a hospital, explain that doctors and nurses work in shifts, all day and all night. Children are amazed that while they're sleeping, there are people working and caring for the community.
Point out how people who work have specialized knowledge about what they do.	Explain that many people go to college or are trained in other ways for their work. Stress the importance of education and how it will prepare them to do all kinds of work. Describe the hard work that artists, athletes, professionals, and others must do to prepare for their work.
Together, make puppets of community workers or other professionals.	It's easy to find instructions for these on the internet. Then, play with the puppets together, imagining situations that illustrate what those professionals do.

Read about different careers in books such as these:

Career Day by Anne Rockwell

The Grasshopper and the Ants (various authors)

If I Could Have Any Job . . . What Would It Be? by Christina Weimer

Jobs on a Farm by Nancy Dickmann

Careers in My Neighborhood by Maria Koran

Helping Hats by Regina C. Brown

There are many websites that offer activities that children can do to learn about community workers and other professions, including biographies of notable people and their work.

Teaching young children about the value of work also helps them make a smoother transition into higher grades in school, where homework and schoolwork are important for keeping up with the lessons. Children should also understand that the work involved in taking care of their homes and possessions is a part of life. You can teach this through chores at home that your child can help with or do, such as cleaning a room, folding clothes or towels, helping at mealtime, or contributing in other ways.

And always remember that children learn to value work based on what they see and hear from the adults around them, so be sure to talk about that do-nothing grasshopper and those hardworking ants!

The Value of Hard Work

by Joshua, Naval Aviator

When I was 12 years old, my parents introduced me to skiing. I loved it. We went every few weeks over the winter, and my skills grew; however, I quickly realized that I'd rather snowboard than ski. So, that spring, I asked my parents to buy me a snowboard. Since they'd just bought me skis in the past six months, they said if I wanted a snowboard, I'd have to pay for it myself.

So, I figured out how to get a job as a paperboy for my local paper. At first, I did substitute work for a friend, but eventually, I got my own route: 49 papers to deliver every morning by 6:30 a.m., 7 days a week, 365 days a year, rain or shine. I lived in Oregon, so it was mostly rain! Every day, for the rest of the year, I woke up at 5:30 a.m., loaded my bag with newspapers, and rode my bike around the neighborhood, delivering the paper. Sometimes, I was sick and couldn't go to school, but I still did my paper route. Sometimes, I didn't want to get up, but I still did my paper route. Sometimes, I wanted to stay the night at a friend's house, so I'd have to get up even earlier so I could ride my bike home and do my paper route.

Eventually, I saved enough money and bought a new snowboard, boots, and snow clothing. I also saved enough money for a season pass so I could take a bus to the mountain and snowboard on one or both days every weekend.

Through this endeavor, I learned the value of working hard to get what you want. I learned the value of determination and not making excuses. I learned that it's better to earn something than to have it given to you. These are all principles that I've carried with me into adulthood, and they've helped me to be successful. I've also been continuously employed ever since!

The World at Their Fingertips

*All the world is a laboratory to the
inquiring mind.*

—Martin H. Fischer

What an amazing opportunity young learners have in the twenty-first century! Technology has opened doors to the world, and it's brought opportunities to work in a competitive global economy at the touch of a button. Many jobs available today didn't even exist ten or twenty years ago. I can only imagine the learning and work opportunities our children will have!

To empower our young learners to be successful in that future, we must find ways to bring the world into their everyday lives. We need to help children learn how people, places, and cultures around the world are both alike and different. Social studies education is so much more important than ever before because children can now affect, and be affected by, events and people in every corner of the world.

The National Council on Social Studies Standards lists 10 major social studies themes:

1. Culture

2. Time, Continuity, and Change

3. People, Places, and Environments

4. Individual Development and Identity

5. Individuals, Groups, and Institutions

6. Power, Authority, and Governance

7. Production, Distribution, and Consumption

8. Science, Technology, and Society

9. Global Connections

10. Civic Ideals and Practices

While these topics may seem advanced, there are ways to teach each of them at a level appropriate for young learners, through experiences provided by teachers and families.

Students can learn by seeing pictures and meeting people and by talking with each other about similarities and differences. For example, children can learn that most people have homes; eat; work; have families; and have similar needs, wants, and feelings. They can learn that in some places, people's homes and clothes may look different; they may eat different foods based on what's available; they may have different kinds of jobs that are related to where they live; and their families may look very different.

Families can help children with these ideas by showing interest, acceptance, and joy when seeing situations different from their own. You can build on your child's questions and interests, beginning with the world around them, such as with family, at school, and with friends. You can gradually expand your child's circle to greater communities, including their city, county, state, country, and world. Start by simply talking about your child's immediate friends and their friends' families as well as what happens every day. Extend your child's knowledge with picture books or children's periodicals about current events. Use maps and globes to expand your child's understanding of where you live, of the larger community, and of the world.

For children in primary grades, it's important to read nonfiction books that include informational text features, such as a table of contents, captioned pictures, sidebars, and a glossary. This experience will prepare your child to learn to read such books independently to better understand the world—from the history of their community to the traditions of cultures on the other side of the world.

There are many wonderful resources for teaching the 10 social studies themes to young children. Here are some favorite social studies books for young learners; they are colorful, visual, and easy to understand:

- *Culture and Diversity* by Marie Murray
- *Families in Many Cultures* by Heather Adamson
- *Clothes in Many Cultures* by Heather Adamson

The following books are a part of a classic series by Ann Morris:

- *Bread, Bread, Bread*
- *Families*
- *Hats, Hats, Hats*
- *Loving*
- *On the Go*
- *Shoes, Shoes, Shoes*
- *Tools*
- *Work*

Other available resources are cultural programs offered by libraries, cultural or ethnic fairs and events, restaurants that offer cultural foods, and museums.

Providing children with rich social studies experiences can be accomplished through one of the greatest gifts we can give our children: our time. This includes talking with them about what they see, encouraging them to draw and/or write about their experiences, and helping them take photographs and create a scrapbook or journal. It also includes travel, whether exploring your own community or visiting others near and far—or even "traveling" through time and space through shared books.

In these ways and others, we must give our children the world—for they are the future citizens and leaders who will shape it!

Love of Travel

by Adria, Professor and CPA

Traveling and seeing new places is a passion that was instilled in me by my parents when I was young. The first big trip our family took was to Washington, D.C., since my mom had an important meeting there. Flying for a family of six was not an option, so we took a road trip! I remember my mother asking our principal if we could be out of school for a week so we could take this historic trip to Washington, D.C., to learn. That exceptional principal said that there was no better learning than through travel and approved our absences.

We stopped at new places along the way, learning about history, cultures, geography, geology, and more. There was so much to see when we got to Washington, D.C., such as the Lincoln Memorial, the Smithsonian Museum, and Arlington National Cemetery, to name a few places. Ever since that trip, we've gone on similar road trips, which has fostered my love for traveling. I also continued traveling as I grew older, with trips to Europe and many cruises.

As a mom, I'm ready to share my love of traveling with my children, to show them the many beautiful places in the world.

Section III

Going to School

Education is key to unlocking the world, a
passport to freedom.

—Oprah Winfrey

Learning Routines and Routines to Learn

Getting organized in the normal routines
of life and finishing little projects you've
started is an important first step toward
realizing larger goals.

—Joyce Meyer

An invaluable survival strategy for parents and teachers of young children is the establishment of daily and weekly routines.

For young children, the concept of time can be difficult, and pictorial representations help them understand the order in which things happen. To help your child learn and remember the daily routines that occur between waking up and bedtime, use pictures, which you can cut out, draw, or take with a camera. This is also an effective way to teach ordinal numbers (*first*, *second*, *third*, and so on) as well as sequencing and time concepts.

Adults like to know what's going to happen when we plan our day. If there are changes, we like to know in advance so we can adapt our schedules. This is just as important for young children. As adults, we sometimes take for granted that our youngsters will adjust and go along with us. But that adjustment occurs much more smoothly when they're prepared for what's going to happen during their day and they have some choices in their routine.

Giving your child the opportunity to make choices and decisions within the daily routine fosters responsibility and sharing.

If you know the family's routine is going to change, sharing that information with your child is always a good idea. Young children can be resilient when given a heads-up, or what is sometimes call an *advance organizer*. Tell children what will happen through the day and to prepare them for changes, such as when they are to be picked up early, when they have a doctor's appointment, or when someone else is going to pick them up after school. As another example, weekends usually involve routines that are different than weekdays for families, so it helps to prepare children by telling them exactly what will be different.

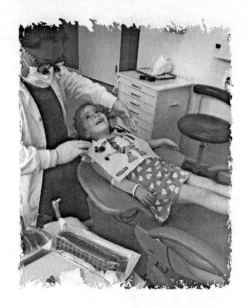

It's also a good idea to let your child help you establish the family's routines. Giving your child the opportunity to make choices and decisions within the daily routine fosters responsibility and sharing. On laundry day, for example, asking your child to help sort colors from whites not only supports the development of responsibility and teaches your child that they can make valuable contributions to the family, but it also helps them learn sorting and classifying skills, which are important in math, reading, and science.

I've found that wherever our daily routines take us, we can find opportunities for teaching and learning. For example, just talking with your child about what you see in the environment will help them build oral language vocabulary, which is an important prereading skill. You can also strengthen important foundational math skills by grouping nearby rocks into sets of five, sorting leaves into different shapes or colors, grouping sticks into tens like tally marks, and whatever else you can imagine!

Plan for moments when you know your child may have to do some waiting, for example, at the doctor's office. Pack a small bag with books, a notebook, and crayons. Make use of any wait time to encourage creativity and learning. Doing something together during this time will strengthen your bond and make the time fly, too!

Families today have complex and very full schedules before, during, and after school. Established routines make for smoother transitions and will help your child prepare mentally for the day and what is to come, while providing frameworks in which creative learning can occur.

So, whether you're learning a routine or creating a routine for learning, think of it as an opportunity to spend quality time with your child—you'll also create wonderful memories of early childhood.

My Love for Animals

by Johnna, Behavior Analyst

I was in kindergarten when my family moved from the town of Woodbridge, New Jersey, to a three-acre lot in Millstone, New Jersey, because my mother wanted a horse. The first horse eventually led to another horse, and then to ponies, pigs, cows, donkeys, goats, sheep, ducks, turkeys, and a llama. We also had cats and dogs. All the animals my parents had were rescued—all of them.

My parents started a small petting zoo and pony-ride business, and my twin sister and I, from an early age, were responsible for helping take care of the animals. I remember having to wake up early before school to feed the animals and then coming home at night after school to feed them all again. My sister and I worked as a team to make sure they had water and were always taken care of.

Fast forward 20 years, and we currently have two dogs and two cats that are part of our family. They were literally rescued off the streets. I can proudly say that both my son and my daughter have learned from a very young age to be kind, compassionate, and gentle to all animals. I find it endearing that they love reading books about and looking at pictures of animals, and they know how to care for their pets. I know that the love they have for animals and the gentleness they show in caring for them have been stepping stones for the compassion, maturity, and responsible nature they exhibit today.

I think growing up with animals and having that responsibility from an early age helped shape who I am today, and my experiences have trickled into how I parent. It's important to me that my children have a deep love and respect for all creatures and understand the responsibility that comes along with caring for these precious lives.

Kindergarten Readiness: Physical and Social/Behavioral Indicators

Education is not preparation for life;
education is life itself.

—John Dewey

What is kindergarten readiness? To a kindergarten teacher, it means that children entering kindergarten are well prepared—physically, socially (that is, how they behave and relate to others—both adults and peers), and academically—to participate positively in class and learn the many concepts and skills that will be taught. To a family, it means, "Is my child ready for kindergarten?"

Most of you know that early childhood education is critical for later school success. But you may not know which social/behavioral and early academic kindergarten-readiness abilities and knowledge your child should have by the time they are old enough to enter kindergarten.

Because there are quite a few indicators of kindergarten readiness, this chapter will focus on physical and social/behavioral (or nonacademic) indicators, and the next chapter will focus on academic indicators.

Physical and Social/ Behavioral Indicators	What Families Can Do
Your child has the ability to listen to others.	<ul><li>Read aloud to your child every day, starting with one page at a time.</li><li>Encourage your child to listen to what you're saying without interrupting.</li><li>Show what it means to listen to others by fully paying attention to your child and asking questions about their interests.</li></ul>
Your child can communicate their needs.	<ul><li>When your child seems to have a problem or wants something, encourage them to explain how they feel; for example:<ul><li>"I'm tired."</li><li>"My finger hurts."</li><li>"I need help with this puzzle."</li></ul></li><li>Encourage your child to speak in complete sentences: "I would like a cheese cracker, please."</li></ul>
Your child can state their own name as well as the names of family members.	<ul><li>Help your child understand that everyone has a name, including mom, dad, brothers or sisters, and other family members.</li><li>Practice saying and spelling family names.</li></ul>
Your child obeys simple rules, such as stand in line and share with others.	<ul><li>Read your child books about school, following rules, and sharing, such as *Know and Follow Rules* by Cheri J. Meiners and *The Berenstain Bears* and *The Golden Rule* by Stan Berenstain and Jan Berenstain.</li><li>Talk to your child about how easy it is to follow school rules; for example:<ul><li>"Stand in line, just like we do at the grocery store."</li><li>"Follow rules, just like Mommy follows traffic rules when she's driving."</li><li>"Share, just like you share your favorite cup with your brother."</li></ul></li></ul>

Physical and Social/ Behavioral Indicators	What Families Can Do
Your child follows instructions.	◆ Regularly give your child one-step directions; for example: ◇ "Please pick up your towel." ◇ "Say thank you to Grandma." ◇ "Stand next to me." ◆ Introduce two-step directions during your daily routine; for example: ◇ "Please pick up your towel and put it in the basket." ◇ "Put the napkin next to the plate, and put the spoon on top of the napkin."
Your child can engage in an activity until it's completed.	◆ Have your child play a game until it is finished. ◆ Help your child with a construction activity, such as blocks, and see it through until it is completed. ◆ Show your child how to clean up their toys after using them and put them away.
Your child can work independently on an age-appropriate task.	◆ Don't help your child with everything. ◆ Encourage your child to work independently as they do puzzles, look through books, color in a coloring book, create art projects, and so on.
Your child demonstrates gross motor skills. (The term gross motor skills refers to the ability to control large muscles, such as those in the arms and legs.)	◆ Have your child practice skipping; bouncing, kicking, and throwing a ball; swinging on a swing; and balancing on a curb or low balance beam. ◆ Encourage your child to try jumping rope, dancing, or gymnastics.

Physical and Social/ Behavioral Indicators	What Families Can Do
Your child demonstrates fine motor skills and eye-hand coordination. (The term fine motor skills refers to the ability to control small muscles, especially those in your child's fingers and hands.)	✦ Have your child practice cutting straight lines, and then simple shapes, with scissors and newspapers. ✦ Ask your child to string small beads or glue pasta on paper. ✦ Encourage your child to practice throwing and catching a ball.
Your child can manage their own clothes.	✦ Have your child regularly practice using zippers, buttons, and snaps. ✦ Encourage your child to practice putting on their clothes independently.
Your child works and plays well with other children.	✦ Point out how you take turns and share when you play with your child. ✦ Let your child play regularly with other children, and observe how they interact. ✦ Take your child to a children's park, museum, or playground; allow them to interact with other children and share toys or equipment.
Your child can separate from you.	✦ Explain to your child that all children go to school and are picked up afterward. ✦ When your child gets dropped off and picked up after visiting with other family members, point out that this is what will happen at school. ✦ Visit a school, and let your child see all the happy children in a kindergarten classroom.

Remember, this is not a checklist of things that suddenly happen when a child turns four or five. Many of these abilities begin to develop from a very early age as you interact with your baby and toddler, by talking, singing, and reading.

If you regularly spend time talking with your child, playing games that promote good literacy and numeracy habits, and supporting the development of the abilities listed above, you will help your child enjoy kindergarten from the moment they enter. You'll also be creating a strong foundation for learning throughout their school years.

Love and Compassion

by Mary, Senior Administrative Assistant

My parents raised us in a household of love. During my childhood, what I admired most was that my mother was a very compassionate person. There were six of us in my family, and I remember her very giving and helpful nature.

One example stands out in my mind. A friend had told my mother about a lady who needed work badly. The lady had no phone, so my mother asked for her address. I remember going to the lady's house in our station wagon, with all my siblings. We lived in Mission, Texas, and we soon found ourselves driving to an impoverished neighborhood. When we arrived, my mother asked us to wait in the station wagon, and she went to knock on the door. A very frail-looking lady answered the door.

My mother hired the lady, and every week, my mother would go to the lady's house to pick her up because she had no car. The lady had a little boy named Juanito, and she would bring him to our house, and we would play with him. He was happy to be at our house. During the holidays, our mom told us that we should do something nice for Juanito and his mother, so we all selected a little gift for him. My mother prepared some food, and we went to the lady's house to deliver gifts and food. My siblings and I were startled to see that the house had no electricity—the lady only had candles. I can still remember the dark and the glow of the candles in her house. My mother truly knew that they had very little.

My mother had six kids, and she worked hard to make ends meet. She made my dad's paycheck last for all of us. Mom fed us, clothed us, and provided a wonderful and caring family home, and she still found time to help people and share what we had.

This compassion and love for others has transferred to my siblings and now to my daughters. One became a teacher and the other a social worker, and they have the same empathy and compassion as my mother. I've also carried it into my work with people. I've worked in the criminal justice system, in a school system, and have helped others make connections to agencies when they've been in need. We've all carried my mom's nurturing love for people. I'm so much like her, and as I think about her in retrospect, I know I'll continue to do my part helping people and honoring my mother's legacy.

Kindergarten Readiness: Academic Indicators

Education is the most powerful weapon which you can use to change the world.

—Nelson Mandela

Now that we've focused on the physical and social/behavioral indicators of kindergarten readiness, it's time to talk about the academic indicators.

The list below includes many of the early academic indicators of kindergarten readiness. It's by no means comprehensive, but it will provide you with an understanding of what will be expected of your child as well as offer tips to help you prepare them for a successful transition to kindergarten.

Academic-Readiness Indicator	What Families Can Do
Your child listens to and understands stories.	+ Begin to read books to your child, even as an infant. + Read the complete story first, for enjoyment, without interruptions. + During additional readings, ask questions about the story and encourage your child to ask questions. + Let your child turn the pages, showing they know it's a story. + Gradually introduce longer books that require more patience and focus.

Academic-Readiness Indicator	What Families Can Do
Your child can retell stories that have been read to them or tell original stories.	✦ Have your child reread a familiar book and try to retell it. ✦ Read nursery rhymes together, and encourage your child to retell them. ✦ Provide puppets or flannel board cutouts that your child can use to retell the stories.
Your child can find matching objects.	✦ Have your child practice matching objects, such as socks from the laundry, pencils or pens, earrings, and food cans in the pantry.

Your child can sort objects by their attributes: color, shape, size, and function, such as things that roll and things they can write with.	✦ Once your child can match objects, encourage them to practice sorting items into categories, such as
	  ◇ Color: Find all the blue shirts, silver coins, and red blocks.
	  ◇ Size: Put big bath towels in one stack and small hand towels in another.
	  ◇ Shape: Find all the round objects in the room.

Your child can identify words that rhyme.	✦ Talk about how some words rhyme: that is, the last part of the words sounds the same. ✦ Have your child find the rhyming words in nursery rhymes. For example, *Jill* and *hill* rhyme in "Jack and Jill;" *Humpty* and *Dumpty* rhyme in "Humpty Dumpty;" and *dock* and *clock* rhyme in "Hickory Dickory Dock." ✦ Play rhyming word games, such as "I know a word that rhymes with *house*. . . . It is a little animal. . . . It is a . . . *mouse*!"
Your child can identify patterns.	✦ Point out patterns as you go about your day, such as patterns in clothing, in plants along a street, and in books you read. ✦ Play pattern-guessing games by arranging objects in a pattern (for example, two red, one blue; two red, one blue), and ask your child to identify the pattern.

Academic-Readiness Indicator	What Families Can Do
Your child can name colors.	✦ Discuss the names of the colors; show how some colors can be made by combining other colors (for example, red and white make pink). ✦ Read books about colors, such as *The Color Kittens* by Margaret Wise Brown and *A Color of His Own* by Leo Lionni. ✦ Use watercolors to paint, and ask your child to mix colors and name them. ✦ Ask your child to name the colors around them, such as in their room, on their clothes, and in the crayon box.
Your child can identify some letters and numbers.	✦ Help your child start to distinguish letters in simple words that they often see written. Begin with the letters in their name. ✦ Point out numbers on everything, such as on money, clocks, signs, phones, and the TV remote.
Your child begins to understand that letters stand for the sounds they hear in words.	✦ Talk about sounds for some of the letters in your child's name, in books, and in other words that they often see during the day. ✦ Write your child's name and other simple words on a sheet of paper or a dry erase board to show how letters form words. ✦ Use magnetic letters on a refrigerator to make real and nonsense words, and sound them out with your child.
Your child recognizes some signs.	✦ Ask your child to "read" words seen during their daily routine, such as *stop* on the stop sign, *walk* at a crosswalk, *gas* at a gas station, and the names of favorite stores or restaurants.
Your child begins to recognize some high-frequency words.	✦ Have your child point out words, such as *the*, *a*, *an*, *and*, *I*, *me*, *is*, *was*, *are*, *go*, and *stop*, that they see often as you read books together. ✦ Write high-frequency words on index cards, and play word games, such as a memory matching game, with your child.

Academic-Readiness Indicator	What Families Can Do
Your child begins to "write" by scribbling; drawing; or imitating letters, numbers, forms, or shapes.	✦ Give your child paper and writing tools in a shoebox that they can use to begin to write, draw, or create shapes. ✦ Give your child a paintbrush and a bowl of water to "paint" on the sidewalk or driveway. (Talk about evaporation as their creations disappear.)
Your child understands how numbers are used.	✦ Show your child how numbers are used in everyday life, such as to count items, to keep track of money, distance, weight, and length; and to measure amounts used in cooking.
Your child can count to 20.	✦ Look for opportunities to count items aloud for and with your child, such as setting the table, sorting clothes, measuring ingredients, and organizing toys. ✦ Encourage and help your child to count objects they see during the day, such as stairs, cups of water, and streetlights.
Your child understands how some words are opposites: *up* and *down*, *big* and *little*, *tall* and *short*, *quiet* and *loud*, and *light* and *heavy*.	✦ Point out examples of opposites that you see. ✦ Play an opposite-guessing game: "The opposite of *day* is . . . *night*!"

Remember, while kindergarten-readiness skills are important and will contribute to a strong foundation for future academic success, the activities that lead up to kindergarten readiness should be enjoyable for your child. Make them fun family times and part of your daily routine so that your child begins to view learning as a positive and natural experience.

Cooperate to Graduate

by Stephanie, Senior Writer

My father was a brilliant man. He transitioned from a career in Army Intelligence to the Defense Intelligence Agency at the Pentagon before I was born. He graduated from the National War College, and over time, medals and many certificates of commendation were hung on what he jokingly referred to as his "I love me" wall. When he later received the first of several high civilian honors for his work with U.S. Special Operations Command, I was able to be there. *That's my dad*, I remember thinking. He loved his country, and he was a proud, devoted, and steadfast servant until the end of his life.

He was also a very cerebral, high-octane guy, trying to navigate a whole other life in the suburbs with three kids. My dad had an amazing vocabulary, and he had a full collection of sayings that he was fond of throwing around.

"Cooperate to graduate."

"If you sign your name, it better mean something."

"Stop sniveling."

"You better suit up and show up."

What does that mean? I remember thinking more than once as a bewildered kid. As a parent myself, I now realize that he was likely stumped and didn't know how else to respond to whatever sibling squabble or school problem we were dealing with—a very different kind of "intelligence." For me, he reserved the super-charged "You're the oldest!" or "You have executive ability!" I may have been confused, but I knew that his expectations were very high and that I'd better figure things out "toot sweet"!

My dad gave me parameters. He pushed me to do my best. I pushed back as a teen. We butted heads. But at the end of the day, he respected my individual freedom to make choices. When I called home one night, not long after I went off to college, saying I didn't know whether to rush a sorority or audition for the fall mainstage play (both events fell on the same night!), he asked me what I would regret the most if I didn't give it a try. His question made things crystal clear for me: in my heart, I knew I was completely drawn to the theater. My mom was the person that I had hoped to talk to that night, but it was my dad who helped me gain clarity.

The older I get, the more I realize that love has so many different languages. My dad had a tremendous belief in me when I was growing up, even though his words for it often went over my head. When I look back on my childhood and some of my interactions with him, it's almost as if they were designed as *aha!* moments for me as an adult. I hear his voice, and I know that whatever I'm up against, somehow, some way, I'll figure it out because that's what he taught me to do: if you suit up, show up, and sign your name with everything you've got; you cooperate to graduate (just don't snivel . . .).

Preventing Learning Loss

The world is the true classroom. The most rewarding and important type of learning is through experience, seeing something with our own eyes.

—Jack Hanna

Breaks from school like winter break or summer vacation can impact student learning and progress. Over time, these learning losses add up, and the academic achievement gap widens. Educators know that children being able to read at grade level by third grade is critically important. Continuing to learn during these breaks is essential to keep children on track, not only for that milestone but also for others—including high school graduation and college enrollment.

The following are some ideas of what you can do to help your child continue to learn over the summer.

1. **Read books daily**. Research shows that books that are "just right" for children (those that aren't frustratingly hard or super-easy) make the best learning experiences.

2. **Talk with your child about their daily experiences**. Encourage your child to draw a picture about their day and write a caption for it or write about it if your child is older.

3. **Use your local public library** to help develop a love of reading and learning. There are many resources at a library: books, technology access, research areas, fun learning activities, and events.

4. **Choose a fun and engaging weekly read-aloud book**. Read a chapter aloud every night, with different family members taking turns reading paragraphs or sentences or as characters in the book. While reading together, here are a few ways to enhance your child's reading skills:

   - Encourage your child to use their imagination by making mental pictures of what they hear. Discuss the differences between their mental pictures and the illustrations.

   - With a younger child, point out letters in the book, and tell your child the letter names and sounds. If your child is slightly older and a beginning reader, point out sight words.

   - Point out rhyming words in the book or words that begin with the same letter.

   - Discuss the book's characters—their names, what they look like, what they're wearing, and what they do. Describing and categorizing are important skills in both reading and math.

   - After reading a story, discuss the setting, the plot, and the main idea.

   - Ask your child questions about what's happening as you're reading the story. Comprehension of the text is an important skill for children to learn.

5. **Take advantage of free summer programs**. Many communities have free summer concerts, parks and recreation events, and farmer's markets. These are all experiences that your child can describe orally or in written form to develop their language skills.

6. **Make every outing a learning opportunity**. Even your grocery store can be a world of wonder, filled with colors, shapes, words, and numbers. Provide questions and other opportunities for your child to learn from the world around them. For example, when you're at a park, encourage your child to explore and identify items, such as:

   - different colors of flowers, shrubs, trees, or other plants

   - geometric shapes and letters in the park, such as the square of a concrete sidewalk and the letter *U* in a park swing

   - leaves (Try sorting them according to similarities, such as color or shape.)

   - types of plants at the park (Read about them online or in books, if your child is older.)

7. **Allow your child to use age-appropriate technology** and high-quality digital learning content, such as top-rated educational applications, on a computer, tablet, or smartphone. Digital books and games can provide excellent learning opportunities for young children when used properly. But keep in mind that time on a device should be managed based on the child's age and should not replace the above activities.

For more wonderful learning suggestions, visit the website for Reading Rockets, a national multimedia literacy initiative. This free website has a wonderful selection of resources as well as a summer reading guide.

Breaks from school don't have to mean learning loss. They can be times of powerful learning for children if we engage them in a wide variety of learning activities. The ideas I've shared are simple yet important experiences that can lead to a love of learning and a growing vocabulary—both crucial for academic success.

Imagine if every book your child opens could be an exciting field trip: your child could go to the moon and beyond, swim below the oceans and through a coral reef, or travel deep into the past or far into the future.

The time and thought that you invest in learning will repay itself many times over, not just at the beginning of the next school year, but in all the school years to come.

My Family's Learning Ritual

by Merlinda, Professional Development Specialist

When my kindergarten class ended each afternoon, my mother would pick me up and take me home, where delicious homemade snacks would be waiting. Each day as I ate, my mother would empty my satchel and say, "Tell me about your day at school. Start at the beginning and tell me all the things you did and heard and learned." Thus began what was to become a family ritual.

My mother would always prompt me with questions. "What is the first thing you did when you got there?" she would ask. "And did you read as well to your teacher as you did last night when you practiced with me?" I would assure her that I had, and the conversation would continue until I had shared every piece of work in my school bag and related my school day in its entirety to her.

When my father arrived home from work, my mother and I would repeat the afternoon's ritual for him. As the years went on, I described math lessons as my mother or father would say, "Explain that again. I don't remember learning this when I was in school."

In the upper grades and high school, I explained parts of speech and literary analyses. I recounted historical events and the roles that people played in those events. I demonstrated how to use reference resources and reduce fractions, and I stepped through the scientific method— always starting at the beginning and retelling everything I heard, did, and learned.

When my two brothers came along, two years and then four years after me, my parents continued the family ritual, but instead, all three of us would start at the beginning and tell everything we heard, did, and learned that day. My brothers ended up hearing about concepts that were two or more years ahead of what was being covered in their classes, and in turn, this helped accelerate their learning. My job was to correct misunderstandings and explain how my brothers' learning was connected to what I was learning. My part also included checking my brothers' homework. "Listen to your sister as she checks your homework so you can get smarter like her," my parents would say. Reviewing their work reinforced concepts for me, so I benefitted from helping my brothers, too.

My parents' persistent and consistently detailed queries inspired my brothers and me to review and reflect on our learning every day, and their amplified vocal admiration encouraged rich retellings. My brothers and I have no doubt: our parents were the smartest people we will ever know.

Going to School: The Learning Continues

> In some parts of the world, students are going to school every day. It's their normal life. But in other parts of the world, we are starving for education . . . it's like a precious gift. It's like a diamond.
>
> —Malala Yousafzai

Children's engagement is crucial in learning, and choices in their own learning help foster their understanding of the world around them. As children go to school, teachers and parents should work together to ensure a smooth transition for children. There should be clear expectations and understanding for what they will encounter in school, and choices should be provided for children in their home and school activities to promote school engagement.

The first few weeks of school are challenging as students find themselves transitioning to school, learning new rules, and developing responsibilities in a new grade level.

There are many tips and strategies that parents can use to help their children with the transition from learning and playing at home to learning at school. Here are a few favorite ideas.

Suggestions	Tips and Examples
Allow your child to create a special study space where they can study or read and focus on school learning topics.	In the space, provide a table and chair, books, pencils, crayons, pens, markers, and paper. Use shoeboxes or small containers for organizers, and urge your child to create labels for their supplies.
Help your child organize their days by providing an hour-by-hour day calendar.	Encourage your child to fill it with their daily schedule by drawing or writing on it. This gives your child a clear visual of their day at school, helps them feel creative, and increases their sense of ownership and having choices.
Positively support your child's efforts by asking about their day or activities.	Make this a routine, and soon you won't have to ask; they will automatically share highlights of their day. Share with your child what you did that day as well.
Read and sing to your child.	Introduce new books and songs, and review the ones your child knows.
Take advantage of the local library.	Make sure you and your child have current library cards to check out books.

Each night, help your child prepare for the next day with activities such as these:

- Let your child set out what they will eat for breakfast. Or, help your child make choices by writing a breakfast menu for the week.
- Help your child lay out clothes, shoes, and socks for the next school day.
- Designate a box, crate, or hanging organizer for lunch boxes and backpacks. Have your child decorate it using pictures cut from magazines, or by drawing on it.
- If your child is taking a lunch, offer a few foods to choose from. If your child is purchasing lunch, encourage them to help you prepare their lunch money.

Sustaining learning throughout the school year poses many challenges. Children have their ups and downs just as adults do. Important in learning, though, is that children feel ownership of what they're learning and why they're learning it. As a former teacher, I can remember getting so involved in covering all the goals that I forgot that the children didn't always know the goals.

Help your child make the connections between school learning concepts. Here are a few examples:

- If your child is learning about recycling at school, talk about what you can do at home to help with recycling. Let your child help you create a family recycling project.

- Perhaps in class, your child is learning about composing numbers ($0 + 5 = 5$; $1 + 4 = 5$; $2 + 3 = 5$; $3 + 2 = 5$; $4 + 1 = 5$; $5 + 0 = 5$). At home, encourage them to practice number facts, using materials around the house, such as pasta, dry beans, pencils, buttons, or anything else you can think of.

- After a school orientation, be sure to bring home a copy of the teacher's long-range goals in each subject for your child's class so that you know what's being taught at school and can prepare to support your child at home. If copies of the class's goals aren't offered, ask your child's teacher to send you one.

As your child goes to school, it's an exciting time for all, and it should be a partnership of learning between the home and the school.

Small World, Big Dreams

by Sunil, Business Executive

My story is like many others, as I am a first-generation immigrant to the United States. As a young child of two, my parents left me with our extended family in Mumbai, India, as they journeyed ahead to make a new home for us in America. They came to the United States, like many others before them, with no money and only the dream of a better life for their family.

Undoubtedly, my parents missed me and their family terribly; however, this sacrifice was necessary for them to provide us with opportunities. My parents' decision to move to the United States gave me a great lesson at an early age, which was that the world could be a small place and accessible to me if I was willing to work hard and make sacrifices.

A year after my parents emigrated, I made my first big move from Mumbai to New York to reunite with them. I now look fondly at pictures of my parents holding me, on top of the Empire State Building. My first experiences in the United States were in Cleveland, Ohio, where my parents initially settled. Soon after, we moved to Atlanta, Georgia, where my dad took a job. We were among the first few Indian families to move to a recently desegregated south.

As an adult, I can see that my childhood shaped my view of the world as a place to explore and one that is amenable to what I have to offer it. After graduating from college in Georgia, I moved to Los Angeles to pursue my first job. When asked at the interview, would I not miss my home, I proudly told them that my parents moved from India so moving across the country wasn't a problem.

My career has taken me to places that my parents could not have even imagined. When my daughter was two and my son was a newborn, I jumped at the opportunity to take a new position and move my family to the United Kingdom. We spent eight years there and were fortunate to experience many cultures and places, including my native India. We are dual citizens of the United States and the United Kingdom, and I hope my children can continue to carry my parents' dream forward and enjoy all the world has to offer.